Resurrection Evidence

Paul De Marco

Copyright 2017

Paul De Marco

All rights reserved

Reproduction in any manner, of the text of this document in whole or in part, in English or in any other language, or otherwise, without the written permission of the author is prohibited.

ISBN : 978-1-326-96593-8

- Books by the same author -

* Fatima 2017

* The Female Disciples of Jesus

* The Teachings of Jesus Christ

* Resurrection Evidence

* Whistle Blower

* Dementia came a calling

* A Fox named White Tip

* Pest Control Nightmares

- Contents -

Chapter

1. What the ancient historians wrote about Jesus
2. Biblical texts and Roman persecution
3. Evolution of the Bible as we know it
4. Ancient source texts of the Bible
5. Discovery of the Dead Sea Scrolls
6. Historical setting at the time of Jesus
7. 1st piece of evidence: The messianic prophecies
8. 2nd piece of evidence: The miracles worked by Jesus
9. Forensic analysis of the death of Jesus
10. 3rd piece of evidence: Inexplicable darkness & earthquake
11. 4th piece of evidence: A guarded tomb found empty
12. 5th piece of evidence: Post resurrection appearances
13. 6th piece of evidence: Disciples prepared for martyrdom
14. Reviewing the evidence - was Jesus the Messiah?

- Introduction -

This book tackles the question that has divided religions for two thousand years and that is whether or not Jesus of Nazareth was divine, or just another one of the prophets.

The resurrection of Jesus has always been a contentious issue and remains the fracture line between the major religions to this day.

He is the only religious figure to have ever claimed to be the son of God and the acid test of his claim is clearly whether or not he rose from the dead.

Our generation has seen unprecedented advances in science, engineering and medicine, where almost everything can now be analysed and its workings understood.

So it's entirely natural for people who are seeking the truth on this question to want firm evidence and this book sets out to prove the divinity of Jesus beyond reasonable doubt, by the scientific analysis of six pieces of evidence.

Two startling events that occurred at the crucifixion have been virtually overlooked by historians and other authors throughout the centuries. One of these is the **inexplicable darkness**, which lasted for a few hours on the Friday afternoon and the other is the **severe earthquake** which struck Jerusalem that same day.

What's intriguing is that both these events were described by ancient historians such as Phlegon and Tertullian and to this day scientists have been unable to offer an explanation for the prolonged period of darkness.

Some have claimed that this was caused by a total solar eclipse, but this book proves scientifically that it couldn't possibly have been caused by either a solar or a lunar eclipse.

The **earthquake** that struck Jerusalem that day and the sixty foot high curtain of the Temple being torn in two are also investigated and geological evidence is given that proves that there was indeed an earthquake at that time.

The book shows that even if the darkness had been caused by a total solar eclipse, the probability of there being both an earthquake and an eclipse on the very day in history that Jesus died, would be **1 in 4.7 billion**.

But the starting point in proving the divinity of Jesus is surely to prove that he indeed lived at the time and place described in the New Testament. For this reason there's a review of the non-biblical writings about him, from eight writers from antiquity, several of whom were non Christian!

These authors include the historians **Josephus**, who was born just four years after Jesus died, **Tertullian**, and the Roman senator **Tacitus**. The writings of **Pliny the Younger**, who was the Roman governor of the province of Bithynia are included, as are the references to Jesus made by Pontius Pilate that were quoted by **Justin the Martyr** around 150 AD. These writings provide irrefutable evidence that Jesus was indeed a genuine historical character.

There follows a brief analysis of the **messianic prophecies** made by King David, who died around 970 BC, as well as the startling prophecies of Isaiah and Micah, through to Zechariah's own prophecy about the Messiah being priced at thirty pieces of silver, written in 520 BC.

The book shows how all these prophecies, made five hundred to a thousand years before he lived, were all fulfilled in the person of Jesus.

The next chapter examines the astonishing **miracles** attributed to Jesus, which are unprecedented in human history, starting with the conversion of between 450 and 690 litres of water into wine at the wedding at Cana.

It details perhaps the greatest miracle of all, the raising of Lazarus to life after he'd been dead for four full days. This act was the final straw for the High Priest Caiaphas, the chief priests and elders of the 69 strong Great Sanhedrin of Jerusalem, who then decided that Jesus simply had to die, to prevent everyone believing in him.

As so much of what we know about Jesus is from biblical texts it's critical that we're confident about their authenticity and accuracy. So the following chapters look at how the bible evolved into its current form and at some of the **ancient source texts** that were used in its compilation.

It also describes the fascinating story of where the papyrus and parchment texts were discovered and investigates just how reliable the current bible texts are when compared to the original source documents.

It describes the **129 years of Roman persecution** of the Church by various Emperors, from the first persecution by Nero in 64 to 68 AD through to the terrible persecution under Galerius and the Tetrarchy from 303 to 313 AD.

It's quite incredible that so much source material survived this period, when the destruction of religious texts was actually mandated by Rome. Some of these atrocities would today be regarded as religious persecution, but others amounted to sheer genocide.

The later schism between King Henry V111 and Rome and the persecution of the Church during the Reformation is also covered in the book.

The fascinating story of the accidental discovery of the ancient **Codex Sinaiticus** by Tischendorf at St Catherine's monastery in 1844 is also described. This codex is dated to around 350 AD and is of immense significance and Tischendorf himself described it as 'the pearl of all my researches.'

The following chapter details the amazing discovery of the **Dead Sea Scrolls** which had been left undisturbed in caves for 1,878 years from 68 AD until they were found by a shepherd trying to rescue a goat from a cave at Qumran in 1947.

The Dead Sea Scrolls allowed researchers for the first time to compare bible texts written in the second century BC, to the Aleppo Codex, the oldest Hebrew bible in existence, from around 930 AD.

Had the writings been corrupted through a thousand years of hand copying texts by many generations of scribes?

The next chapter examines crucifixion and the **medical causes of death** as a result of this common form of capital punishment and it shows that Jesus indeed died at Calvary and that he couldn't possibly have survived his crucifixion.

Another chapter investigates whether or not Jesus rose from the dead and there's an analysis of several hypotheses to explain the **empty tomb** discovered on the Sunday morning.

All the accounts of the **post-resurrection appearances** of Jesus are then analysed in detail.

Then there's a brief outline of the **lives of the apostles** as well as some of the other disciples such as Saint Paul. It shows how they were all prepared for martyrdom, to die promoting the claim that Jesus was the Christ and examines what could possibly have motivated them to do this.

The final chapter pulls the six pieces of evidence together and proves scientifically and by logical deduction that Jesus is the son of God.

This book shows that faith doesn't have to be blind, as there's an abundance of scientific evidence to prove the divinity of Jesus.

It presents a strong challenge to atheists with an open mind, but it will also greatly enrich the knowledge and faith of Christian believers.

- Chapter 1 -
What the ancient historians wrote about Jesus

The majority of people would probably agree that Jesus was a genuine historical character even if they contest his resurrection. Some however even argue that the New Testament writings about Jesus were fabricated and propose that he never actually lived.

The problem with this argument is that it would be necessary to explain away the writings of all the non Christian historians from antiquity who wrote about Jesus.

Flavius Josephus

Arguably one of the greatest historians from antiquity was a Jew named Josephus. Born in Jerusalem in 37 AD, Joseph was raised as a Sadducee, which was one of the two main sects of Judaism and which taught that there was no life after death.

He was a keen student of religion and for several years devoted himself to studying the other branches of Judaism, that of the Pharisees and the Essenes. But at the age of nineteen he broke with family tradition and become a Pharisee, the sect of Judaism that maintains that there is in fact a life after death.

After sporadic uprisings and tensions over high taxation, the Jews began an armed revolt against Roman occupation in 66 AD which resulted in a bloody four year war.

The Jews enjoyed early success in the war, including destroying the Roman garrison at Jerusalem and the 29 year old Joseph joined the rebels soon after this victory.

The Romans brought in a large army from Syria to regain control, but were ambushed and defeated once again at the battle of Beth Horon in 66 AD, suffering 6,000 casualties.

In 67 AD, the Roman general Vespasian was given command of four legions and instructed to regain control of the province of Judea. Vespasian was a highly talented general and twenty four years earlier had been involved in the successful invasion of Britain of 43 AD.

Previous invasions of Britain going as far back as the invasions under Julius Caesar in 55 and 54 BC and that of Claudius in 27 BC had all been spectacular failures.

Vespasian appointed his elder son Titus as second in command and they organised a counter attack on Galilee in which they slowly regained control.

Joseph's men were eventually surrounded near the town of Yodfat (Jotapata) in 67 AD and he was later forced to surrender after a siege lasting 47 days.

After this defeat he defected to the Romans and being a well educated young man, soon became an adviser to Titus himself. During the Roman army's six month siege of Jerusalem in 70 AD, Joseph worked as a translator and was sent to persuade the defenders to give up the fight and to save their lives as well as the temple and the city itself.

However he was seen as a traitor by his former comrades and was unable to negotiate their surrender and was even wounded by one of them by being shot with an arrow.

When the war ended with the destruction of Jerusalem and the annihilation of the Jewish population, Joseph became an historian and wrote for the next thirty years until his death around 100 AD.

Josephus was born only 4 years after the death of Jesus and so many of the people that Jesus had healed, or who had witnessed the miracles, would still have been alive when he was a young man.

He would therefore have had access to people with first hand experience of the miracles themselves and of the spectacular events at the crucifixion and this surely lends weight to the authenticity of his writings.

Two of his notable works were 'Antiquities of the Jews' and 'An apology of Judaism.'

The Antiquities of the Jews is a history of the Jewish people in twenty books and was written in Rome sometime around 93 to 94 AD.

It contains a fascinating passage called the **'Testimonium Flavianum'** in which Jesus is described (Book 18, chapter 3 verse 3).

'Now there was about this time Jesus, a wise man, if it be lawful to call him a man, for he was a doer of wonderful works, a teacher of such men as receive the truth with pleasure. He drew over to him both many of the Jews, and many of the Gentiles. He was the Christ; and when Pilate, at the suggestion of the principal men among us, had condemned him to the cross, those that loved him at the first did not forsake him; for he appeared to them alive again the third day, as the divine prophets had foretold these and ten thousand other wonderful things concerning him; and the tribe of Christians, so named from him, are not extinct to this day.'

So in this text Josephus clearly refers to the crucifixion of Jesus and he also places the time of the crucifixion as being during the rule of Pontius Pilate, which agrees with the gospel accounts.

Tacitus

Tacitus was a Roman senator who lived from around 56 to 117 AD and is regarded as having been one of the greatest historians from ancient times.

One of his acclaimed works was the '**Annals**' which he wrote in 109 AD and in this work Tacitus refers to the Emperor Nero's persecution of Christians in Rome, which began in 64 AD.

Fires had ravaged the city but many of the citizens thought that they'd been started on Nero's orders to give him an excuse for building a grand new palace. Tacitus wrote:

'Consequently, to get rid of the report, Nero fastened the guilt and inflicted the most exquisite tortures on a class hated for their abominations, called Christians by the populace.

Christus, from whom the name had its origin, suffered the extreme penalty during the reign of Tiberius at the hands of one of our procurators, Pontius Pilatus, and a most mischievous superstition, thus checked for the moment, again broke out not only in Judaea, the first source of the evil, but even in Rome, where all things hideous and shameful from every part of the world find their centre and become popular.

Accordingly, an arrest was first made of all who pleaded guilty; then, upon their information, an immense multitude was convicted, not so much of the crime of firing the city, as of hatred against mankind. Mockery of every sort was added to their deaths.

Covered with the skins of beasts, they were torn by dogs and perished, or were nailed to crosses, or were doomed to the flames and burnt, to serve as a nightly illumination, when daylight had expired.

Nero offered his gardens for the spectacle, and was exhibiting a show in the circus, while he mingled with the people in the dress of a charioteer or stood aloft on a car.

Hence, even for criminals who deserved extreme and exemplary punishment, there arose a feeling of compassion; for it was not, as it seemed, for the public good, but to glut one man's cruelty, that they were being destroyed.' (**Annals Book 15, chapter 44**)

From this text it's quite clear that Tacitus felt contempt for Christians and the following points mentioned by him are significant. Firstly that Jesus was executed during the reign of Tiberius Claudius, who we know from many sources, was Emperor from 14 to 37 AD.

Secondly that he was executed by order of Pontius Pilate, who was procurator from 26 to 36 AD. Thirdly, that the 'mischievous superstition' of Christianity had begun in the province of Judea.

Now all these details are in agreement with the gospel writer's accounts of who was in power at the time Jesus lived and died and there's also agreement on where he lived.

Acts of Pilate

Another document in which Jesus was described is 'The Acts of Pilate' or Acta Pilati, which is a text that was incorporated into the apocryphal Gospel of Nicodemus.

The Acta Pilati are an account of the official acts of Pilate from the Praetorium in Jerusalem, which include a communication to the Emperor Tiberius in which he wrote about Jesus.

There's a great deal of controversy over whether or not these writings ever existed and the document in existence today is believed to be a late fourth or early fifth century fabrication. However it's certainly plausible that a document did exist which has subsequently been lost and if the crucifixion of Jesus did occur as recorded in the gospels, then it's likely that Pilate would have reported the incident.

What's intriguing is that reference is made to 'The Acts of Pilate' by certain historians from antiquity long **before** the fourth century AD!

According to the Gospel writings, Pilate's hesitancy in passing the death sentence in the trial had almost sparked rioting in the streets of Jerusalem.

There had also been a major earthquake and an inexplicable period of darkness which lasted for a few hours on the actual day of the crucifixion, which were clearly both newsworthy events.

Also Jesus had worked a great number of miracles over a period of three years, some of which Pilate would have been aware of and he was fully aware that he'd executed a man many believed to be the King of the Jews. After all Pilate even had this notice fixed to the cross!

In addition to this, Pilate and his wife Claudia were so troubled by the events at the crucifixion that they both went into fasting that day, according to the Gospel of Nicodemus.

So clearly all this would have been worthy of mention in a report and you could argue that it would have been remiss of Pilate not to have informed the Emperor of these events.

These happenings would surely have come to his attention sooner or later and records do show that all governors wrote letters to the emperor on a regular basis.

The Acts of Pilate are referred to in the Apology letters of Justin the Martyr, which Justin wrote while living in Rome and which he addressed to the Emperor Antoninius Pius and to the Roman governor Urbicus around 150 AD.

Justin lived from around 100 AD until he was martyred in about 165 AD and in chapter 13 of his **Apology** he wrote:

"Our teacher of these things is Jesus Christ, who also was born for this purpose, and was crucified under Pontius Pilate, procurator of Judaea in the times of Tiberius Caesar; and that we reasonably worship Him, having learned that He is the Son of the true God Himself, and holding

Him in the second place, and the prophetic Spirit in the third, we will prove.

For they proclaim our madness to consist in this, that we give to a crucified man a place second to the unchangeable and eternal God, the Creator of all; for they do not discern the mystery that is herein, to which, as we make it plain to you, we pray you to give heed."

Justin clearly believed that there were records of a communication between Pilate and Tiberius Caesar in the imperial archives because he went on to say the following:

"And the expression, 'They pierced my hands and my feet,' was used in reference to the nails of the cross which were fixed in His hands and feet. And after He was crucified they cast lots upon His vesture, and they that crucified Him parted it among them. And that these things did happen, **you can ascertain from the Acts of Pontius Pilate**." (Chapter 35)

"And that it was predicted that our Christ should heal all diseases and raise the dead, hear what was said. There are these words: 'At His coming the lame shall leap as an hart, and the tongue of the stammerer shall be clear speaking: the blind shall see, and the lepers shall be cleansed; and the dead shall rise, and walk about.' And that He did those things, **you can learn from the Acts of Pontius Pilate**." (Chapter 48)

This is clearly significant as Justin's referral to the Acts of Pilate were part of his defence and it's highly unlikely that he would have invented such a report to the Roman Emperor as he was facing the very real possibility of execution.

Tertullian

Quintus Tertullianus lived from around 160 to 225 AD in Carthage (modern day Tunisia) and one of his works was 'The Apologeticum' which he wrote in 197 AD.

In these writings he made numerous references to Christ and he also described a report made by Pontius Pilate to Tiberius regarding the fact that he had pronounced the unjust sentence of death against an innocent and divine person.

In Apologeticum chapter 5 he wrote that the Emperor Tiberius was so moved by the account of Jesus by Pontius Pilate, that he had wanted to make him one of the Gods of Rome but that this had subsequently been rejected by the senate.

'Tiberius accordingly, in whose days the Christian name made its entry into the world, having himself **received intelligence from Palestine** of events which had clearly shown the truth of Christ's divinity, brought the matter before the senate, with his own decision in favour of Christ. The senate, because it had not given the approval itself, rejected his proposal. Caesar held to his opinion, threatening wrath against all accusers of the Christians.' (**Apologeticum, Chapter 5**)

Later in chapter 21 Tertullian gives a lengthy description of the miracles worked by Christ, as well as his crucifixion and the fact that his tomb was found empty on the third day, despite it being surrounded with a large detachment of guards.

Notice how he also described the **darkness at midday**, which he clearly did not believe was caused by an eclipse and that he referred to this astonishing event being documented in the Roman archives.

'As, then, under the force of their pre-judgment, they had convinced themselves from His lowly guise that Christ was no more than man, it followed from that, as a necessary consequence, that they should hold Him a magician from the powers which He displayed, expelling devils from men by a word, restoring vision to the blind, cleansing the leprous, reinvigorating the paralytic, summoning the dead to life again, making the very elements of nature obey Him, stilling the storms and walking on the sea; proving that He was the Logos of God, that primordial first-begotten Word, accompanied by power and reason, and based on Spirit, that He who was now doing all things by His word, and He who had done that of old, were one and the same.

But the Jews were so exasperated by His teaching, by which their rulers and chiefs were convicted of the truth, chiefly because so many turned aside to Him, that at last they brought Him before Pontius Pilate, at that time Roman governor of Syria; and, by the violence of their outcries against Him, extorted a sentence giving Him up to them to be crucified. He Himself had predicted this; which, however, would have signified little had not the prophets of old done it as well.

And yet, nailed upon the cross, He exhibited many notable signs, by which His death was distinguished from all others. At His own free-will, He with a word dismissed from Him His spirit, anticipating the executioner's work.

In the same hour, too, the light of day was withdrawn, when the sun at the very time was in his meridian blaze. Those who were not aware that this had been predicted about Christ, **no doubt thought it an eclipse. You yourselves have the account of the world-portent still in your archives.**

Then, when His body was taken down from the cross and placed in a sepulchre, the Jews in their eager watchfulness surrounded it with a large military guard, lest, as He had predicted His resurrection from the dead on the third day, His disciples might remove by stealth His body, and deceive even the incredulous.

But, lo, on the third day there was a sudden shock of earthquake, and the stone which sealed the sepulchre was rolled away, and the guard fled off in terror: without a single disciple near, the grave was found empty of all but the clothes of the buried One.

But nevertheless, the leaders of the Jews, whom it nearly concerned both to spread abroad a lie, and keep back a people tributary and submissive to them from the faith, gave it out that the body of Christ had been stolen by His followers.' (**Apologeticum, Chapter 21**)

Seutonius

Chrestus was also mentioned by the Roman historian Suetonius who lived from 69 to 122 AD, in his work 'Life of Claudius.'

Chapter 25.4: As the Jews were making constant disturbances at the instigation of Chrestus, he expelled them from Rome.

The historian and theologian Paulus Orosius also wrote about this expulsion of the Jews from Rome, which he said had happened in 49 AD. This endorses what was written about the expulsion of Jews from Rome in Christian writings, specifically in Acts 18:1:

'After this, Paul left Athens and went to Corinth. There he met a Jew named Aquila, a native of Pontus, who had recently come from Italy with his wife Priscilla, because Claudius had ordered all the Jews to leave Rome.'

Galen

Jesus is also mentioned in the writings of the Roman physician Galen in his work 'De differentiis pulsuum' which was written sometime between 176 and 192 AD.

De differentiis pulsuum (ii, 4) ... in order that one should not at the very beginning, as if one had come into the school of Moses and Christ, hear talk of undemonstrated laws, and that where it is least appropriate.

(iii, 3): One might more easily teach novelties to the followers of Moses and Christ than to the physicians and philosophers who cling fast to their schools.

Lucian

Lucian of Samosata was an anti-Christian satirist living in the second century and he wrote a play entitled 'The passing of Peregrinus' in which he referred to Jesus without actually mentioning him by name. It's thought to have been written around 165 to 175 AD.

11. It was then that he learned the wondrous lore of the Christians, by associating with their priests and scribes in Palestine. And - how else could it be? - in a trice he made them all look like children, for he was prophet, cult-leader, head of the synagogue, and everything, all by himself.

He interpreted and explained some of their books and even composed many, and they revered him as a god, made use of him as a lawgiver, and set him down as a protector, next after that other, to be sure, whom they still worship, the man who was crucified in Palestine because he introduced this new cult into the world.

13. The poor wretches have convinced themselves, first and foremost, that they are going to be immortal and live for all time, in consequence of which they despise death and even willingly give themselves into custody; most of them. Furthermore, their first lawgiver persuaded

them that they are all brothers of one another after they have transgressed once for all by denying the Greek gods and by worshipping that crucified sophist himself and living under his laws.

Pliny the Younger

Pliny the Younger was the governor of the province of Bithynia (Turkey) and he wrote a letter to the Emperor Trajan around 112 AD in which he made reference to Christ.

On Trajan's orders he had begun executing Christians that refused to deny their faith and he wrote to Trajan for assurance and for clarification on the legality of these executions. Pliny clearly had concerns about the enormous number of people he was putting to death during the persecution.

'….. Others of them that were named in the libel, said they were Christians, but presently denied it again; that indeed they had been Christians, but had ceased to be so, some three years, some many more; and one there was that said he had not been so these twenty years.

All these worshipped your image, and the images of our gods; these also cursed Christ. However, they assured me that the main of their fault, or of their mistake was this:

That they were wont, on a stated day, to meet together before it was light, and to sing a hymn to Christ, as to a god, alternately; and to oblige themselves by a sacrament (or oath), not to do anything that was ill: but that they would commit no theft, or pilfering, or adultery; that they would not break their promises, or deny what was deposited with them, when it was required back again; after which it was their custom to depart, and to meet again at a common but innocent meal, which they had left off upon that edict which I published at your command, and wherein I had forbidden any such conventicles.'

In his letter to Trajan, Pliny wrote that the superstition was spreading 'like a contagion.'

'Hereupon I have put off any further examinations, and have recourse to you, for the affair seems to be well worth consultation, especially on account of the number of those that are in danger; for there are many of every age, of every rank, and of both sexes, who are now and hereafter likely to be called to account, and to be in danger; for this superstition is spread like a contagion, not only into cities and towns, but into country villages also, which yet there is reason to hope may be stopped and corrected.'

It would seem highly improbable that all these references to a person named Jesus were completely fabricated, as we have here the writings of politicians, play writes and historians, as well as what was written by the New Testament authors themselves.

In addition to this, several of these authors clearly hated Christians and the person who had started the faith in the first place.

If we are to discount the writings of all these reputable authors and deny that Jesus ever lived, then surely logic would dictate that we must call into doubt the existence of other characters from history mentioned in ancient writings.

What test for accepting the authenticity of historical texts would we then apply?

In summary, there's overwhelming evidence that Jesus was a genuine historical character and that he lived at the time and place described in the gospels and it's also clear that there's consensus among these historians that Jesus was indeed crucified.

- Chapter 2 -
Biblical texts and Roman persecution

As so much of what we know of the life of Jesus is derived from biblical texts we need to look at the credibility of the Bible and ask ourselves just how accurately today's texts reflect what was originally written? In fact where are all the ancient biblical source texts today and how do we even know that they're authentic?

Jewish traditions and beliefs from the Patriarchal period were passed by word of mouth from one generation to the next, but in later history these beliefs were committed to writing, although initially not in any coordinated way.

Defining the range of time the Patriarchal period covered i.e. the period pre-slavery in Egypt, is very difficult due to the lack of firm archaeological evidence.

William Albright the American biblical scholar and archaeologist estimated it to have been from 2100 to 1800 BC but others have placed it around 1950 to 1500 BC.

The Old Testament books were originally written in Hebrew, with the first biblical author believed to have been Moses himself. In fact in the Book of Exodus it actually states that Moses was instructed to write by God.

Exodus 34:27: Then the Lord said to Moses, "Write down these words, for in accordance with these words I have made a covenant with you and with Israel."

There's been much debate over the dating of the earliest writings of the Old Testament, with some scholars dating them to as far back as 1400 BC, but others to around 1250 BC.

Dating the exodus of the Israelites from Egypt has also produced a wide range of dates, with some scholars placing this event at around 1450 BC, but the lack of archaeological evidence for the exodus at this stage means that the date remains subjective.

Malachi is the last book of the Old Testament and is often dated to between 445 and 432 BC. One of the earliest writings in the Bible is believed to be the Song of Moses and Miriam in Exodus chapter 15 and this song celebrated the destruction of the Egyptian army in the Red Sea after Moses had led the Israelites out of Egypt.

Miriam was the sister of Moses and Aaron and it was Miriam that hid her baby brother by the bulrushes of the river Nile in Egypt. On their wanderings in the desert, Moses would chant this song to the men and Miriam chanted it to the women, presumably to keep them motivated.

The first five books of the Old Testament are collectively called 'The Law' or Torah and they're called the Pentateuch in Greek, which translates as the five scrolls. These books have traditionally been attributed to Moses, but there's been debate over how much of them Moses actually wrote himself, as the writings span a considerable period of time and comprise different writing styles.

Some of the writings, such as those in the book of Deuteronomy, were written about Moses, although some have argued that he could have been writing in the third person. The description of the death of Moses in Deuteronomy, which was the last writing of the Torah, was clearly penned by another author!

Deuteronomy 31:24 contains a fascinating verse.

After Moses finished writing in a book the words of this law from beginning to end, he gave this command to the Levites who carried the ark of the covenant of the Lord: "Take this Book of the Law and place it beside the ark of the covenant of the Lord your God."

So this indicates that for a period of time, the Ten Commandments, written on tablets of stone, were actually placed alongside the writings of Moses which had been written on parchment.

The first Temple of Jerusalem had been built by King Solomon and was completed by 957 BC and it encapsulated the religion and traditions of the Israelite nation. However in 586 BC the Babylonians destroyed the city of Jerusalem and its temple and the majority of the Israelite nation was then taken into captivity.

The Israelites had lost their independence, they no longer had a King and they had also lost the most important religious site at which to worship their God.

It's likely that during this difficult period in exile that there was a formalisation of the Hebrew scriptural writings and the priests and scribes are thought to have collated these into the Torah. This would have ensured that the traditions and beliefs could be preserved for all future generations.

The Israelites remained in captivity for 47 years until the fall of the Babylonian Empire in 539 BC, when Cyrus of Persia permitted them to return to Jerusalem. It's no coincidence that construction of the second temple began the very next year in 538 BC and the massive building project was finally completed 23 years later in 515 BC.

The second temple stood for 585 years but was ultimately destroyed by Titus and his four legions in 70 AD and the site is now occupied by the Al-Aqsa Mosque and the Dome of the Rock in Jerusalem.

Although the Old Testament was written in Hebrew, the Aramaic language had gained in popularity and was very commonly spoken at the time of Jesus. In fact many Jews would have been unable to read Hebrew at this time!

But despite Aramaic being the common language in use, the Books of the New Testament were virtually all written in Greek, as this was a commonly spoken international language and the language used by scholars.

The books of the New Testament were written from about 48 AD onwards, or from about 15 years after the death of Jesus and it's thought that Paul's first letter to the Thessalonians, followed by his letter to the Galatians were the first writings of the New Testament and are dated to 48-52 AD.

However some scholars take the view that the epistle of James was written by 50 AD and that it slightly pre-dates Thessalonians and Galatians.

There's been much debate about who wrote the Book of Revelation, either John the Apostle or another person named John who also lived for a time on the Roman penal colony of Patmos, as the two texts have differences in linguistic style and theology.

Irenaeus, Justin Martyr and Tertullian all believed that the apostle wrote both, but Eusebius of Caesarea, Cyril of Jerusalem and John

Chrysostom disagreed with this view. The Book of Revelation was probably written around 95 AD.

Of the gospels, either Matthew or Mark's gospel was written first and both were likely completed between 65 and 70 AD.

Some theologians believe that all the Gospels were written before 64 AD, as none of them mention major historical events including the great fire of Rome of that year, which initiated a terrible persecution by Nero.

None of them record the martyrdom of the apostle James the Less in the spring of 62 AD or the martyrdom of Peter and Paul between 67 and 68 AD.

Similarly, the Jewish Roman war, which culminated in the complete destruction of Jerusalem and the massacre of the majority of the Jewish population in 70 AD, is also not described in the gospels.

However the omission of all these events may simply be because the writers were concerning themselves with the teachings of Jesus, as opposed to documenting historical events.

It's interesting that the martyrdom of James the brother of John, who was killed with a sword on the instruction of Herod Agrippa around 44 AD, is mentioned in the book of Acts.

However the martyrdom of James the Just in 62 AD isn't mentioned, nor are the deaths of any of the other apostles. Also, none of the historical events mentioned above were documented in Acts and for these reasons some scholars believe that this book was written around 62 or possibly 63 AD.

One wonders why the disciples took so long to put quill to papyrus after Jesus died, but it was probably because they were all anticipating the second coming of Jesus to occur within their lifetime. As the years passed and their understanding of his teachings became clearer, they would have realised that this was not the case and that his teachings had to be documented for future generations.

The writings were made on both papyrus and parchment, but during the early days of the Church the writing material most commonly used was papyrus, as it was freely available and far less expensive than parchment. Papyrus had been used from at least as far back as 2000 BC and was the writing material of choice until around 300 AD.

Papyrus is a very tough reed from the Nile valley and the fibrous pith of the plant was the part that was used as a writing material. The pith was cut into strips and arranged vertically with a slight overlap of each strip and the same was done with strips laid horizontally on top and then the two sections were glued together. After being allowed to dry, the sheets of papyrus were polished to give a smooth writing surface.

Most of the papyrus fragments of biblical texts that have so far been discovered have been found in Egypt, where the bone dry climate ensured their preservation.

Leather was far more expensive but more durable than papyrus and it was either made from goat or sheep skin, called parchment, or the higher quality calf skin, known as vellum.

The leather was treated with lime and then polished to give it a smooth surface and the scribes preferred to use this material for their Old Testament scrolls due to its durability, as the scrolls had to be rolled up and unrolled again on a regular basis in the synagogues.

As an example of the costs involved, the skin of one goat would provide only five pages for a codex and so a 250 page codex would require at least 50 sheep or goats!

However leather grew in popularity and was very commonly used from 300 to 1100 AD, when it finally gave way to paper.

It's fascinating that about 85% of the writings at Qumran, the Dead Sea scrolls, were made on leather, despite the fact that this community vacated the site around 68 AD during the Roman Jewish war.

Christian writers seem to have favoured leather from around the beginning of the 4th century and this may have coincided with the Edict of Milan in 313 AD, when Christianity finally ceased to be persecuted throughout the Roman Empire.

In the latter half of the first century, Christian writers gradually evolved from using the scroll to the codex or book format, probably because they were less cumbersome to carry and use. However the Jewish scribes continued to favour the traditional scroll and the Masoretic scribes, which are described later, only moved to the codex as late as 700 AD.

Saint Paul referred to his scrolls in his letter to Timothy and from this short reading we can see that Paul wrote on both papyrus and parchment.

2 Timothy 4:13: 'When you come, bring the cloak that I left with Carpus at Troas, and my scrolls, especially the parchments.'

The apostle John clearly also used papyrus as a writing material, as is clear from **2 John 12**:

'I have much to write to you, but I do not want to use paper and ink.'

Now Luke records in his gospel that a scroll of Isaiah was handed to Jesus to read in the synagogue at Nazareth and this would have been a copy made for the synagogue by one or more of the scribes.

Luke 4:17: The scroll of the prophet Isaiah was handed to him. Unrolling it, he found the place where it is written:

"The Spirit of the Lord is on me, because he has anointed me to preach good news to the poor. He has sent me to proclaim freedom for the prisoners and recovery of sight for the blind, to release the oppressed, to proclaim the year of the Lord's favour."

Then he rolled up the scroll, gave it back to the attendant and sat down. The eyes of everyone in the synagogue were fastened on him, and he said to them, "Today this scripture is fulfilled in your hearing."

Unfortunately no autographed **original manuscripts** have yet been found from either the Old or the New Testament but this is hardly surprising given the age of the documents and the same is true of most writers from ancient times.

There were a series of brutal persecutions of the early Christian church by the Romans and during these times a massive quantity of biblical texts were destroyed.

In fact it's estimated that from the first persecution by Nero in 64 AD, until the Edict of Milan was signed in 313 AD, there were 129 years of persecution against Christians! So for about half of this period Christians faced persecution and ten of the persecutions were widespread throughout the Roman Empire and very severe in nature.

Persecution of Nero

The first state sanctioned persecution of Christians was under the emperor Nero, from 64 to 68 AD and began after a widespread fire had destroyed much of Rome.

According to Tacitus, the fire started on the night of 18th July 64 AD and Seutonius wrote that it raged for six days and seven nights. The cause of the fires is unknown, but it started in the shops around the Circus Maximus and may have been started on the instruction of Nero himself, to give him an excuse for building a grand new palace.

Four out of fourteen districts of Rome were destroyed and seven more were severely damaged with the Emperor's palace and the temple of Jupiter burned to the ground.

In his writings 'the Annals,' Tacitus wrote that Nero blamed the Christians for having started the fires and so began a persecution against them, with the most extreme cruelty being shown.

One of the punishments that Nero introduced was to make Christians wear clothing steeped in heavy wax, before crucifying them. Still alive, they were then set alight, to slowly burn to death in his gardens, so as to illuminate them at special functions he put on.

It's almost certain that both Peter and Paul were martyred during this four year period of persecution, probably in 67 or 68 AD. Crucifixions of Christians were common at this time, but many were martyred in the Colosseum by being thrown to starved wild animals.

Another barbaric method of execution was to tie animal skins to the naked bodies of Christians before throwing them in with packs of starving dogs.

For the first time in history, from the outset of this initial persecution by Nero, a distinction was made between Jews and Christians and thereafter it became an offence to be a Christian, punishable by death. However it was still possible to renounce Jesus in public and to offer a sacrifice to the Roman Gods in order to escape the death penalty.

Eventually there were rebellions against Nero's rule, which began because of discontent over taxation and his power base slipped away from him.

Fearing that he was about to be executed in public, Nero decided to commit suicide and on the 9th of June 68 AD he asked one of his attendants to stab him to death.

As he was dying, the clearly delusional emperor said, "Qualis artifex pereo," which means 'what an artist dies in me.'

Two years after Nero's persecution of Christians ended, the city of Jerusalem and its temple were burned to the ground on 10th August 70 AD and it's impossible to quantify the volume of biblical material lost during this six year period of carnage.

Persecution of Decius

The emperor Decius only ruled from 249 to 251 AD but he ordered a brutal crackdown on Christians and forced them to offer sacrifices to the Roman Gods.

Bishops and priests were rounded up and executed and the lay people were offered the choice of either making sacrificial offerings to the Roman Gods or of facing execution.

The ritual of offering sacrifices included the burning of incense and the act had to be performed in front of a magistrate and witnesses, who would then issue the person with a certificate of compliance called a Libellus.

Jews were however exempt from being forced to offer sacrifices to the Roman Gods and this was the first time in history that legislation had been enacted to force Christians to give up their faith or face execution.

The status of Jews was very different to that of Christians, as Judaism had been awarded '**Religio licita**' status and so it was a permitted religion throughout the empire.

Christianity was regarded not so much as a religion but as a superstition and one that was highly disruptive to society. The Romans approved of the heritage and tradition in other faiths, but they regarded Christians as having turned from the beliefs of their ancestors, the Jews.

Some notable Christians were executed for non compliance during the persecution of Decius, including Pope Fabian, who was martyred on 20th January 250 AD. Alexander of Jerusalem was another victim and is reported to have survived various tortures including being thrown to the beasts, before finally dying in prison in 251 AD.

Decius was killed at the battle of Abrittus in north eastern Bulgaria in June 251 AD while fighting the Goths and his Roman army was massacred as they were trapped in the swamps.

Persecution of Valerian

Valerian ruled from 253 to 260 AD during a period of absolute turmoil in the Roman Empire in both the East and the West. During his war with the Persian King, Shapur I, Valerian initiated a ruthless persecution against Christians, which lasted from the April of 257 until the October of 260 AD.

Again the initial target was the clergy of the church and Stephen, the Bishop of Rome, was beheaded. Saturninus, the Bishop of Toulouse, was tied by his ankles to the tail of a bull and then dragged down stone steps until his skull was crushed.

There were mass executions of lay Christians and Valerian even issued an order for all the clergy in Rome to be executed. Sextus, who had replaced Stephen as the Bishop of Rome, was then killed along with six of his deacons in 258 AD. The Bishop Cyprian was also beheaded and eight of his disciples martyred, but one of the most horrific massacres occurred at Utica, where three hundred Christians were incinerated together in a kiln when they refused to offer sacrifices to the Roman god Jupiter.

But Valerian's reign of terror came to an abrupt end when his army, weakened by an outbreak of plague, was besieged and then defeated by the army of Shapur at Edessa. Valerian was the first Roman Emperor in history to be captured and taken as a prisoner of war, although historians aren't in agreement on exactly how he died.

But it seems clear that he was publically humiliated over a long period of time, possibly even being used as a footstool by Shapur when he mounted his horse. He was ultimately killed, either by being forced to drink molten gold or by being flayed alive, possibly in 264 AD.

Persecution of Galerius and the Tetrarchy

The last major Roman persecution began on 24th February 303 AD and involved the tetrarchy of Diocletian; Maximian, Galerius and Constantius.

Records show that Diocletian and Galerius had argued bitterly over how to deal with the problem of Christians at the Council of Nicomedia, which convened in 302 AD.

Diocletian wanted to exclude Christians from positions of public office, but Galerius wanted to adopt a policy of mass extermination throughout the Roman Empire.

However they finally agreed on four edicts to control the spread of Christianity and the persecution began with the burning of the church in Nicomedia along with its scriptures on 23rd February 303 AD.

The next day an edict mandated the destruction of all scriptures and churches and made it illegal for Christians to meet together and the legal rights of Christians were also withdrawn and many were executed.

The second edict in the summer of 303 AD called for the arrest of all Christian clergy and a third proclamation by Diocletian offered amnesty to clergy if they offered sacrifices to the Roman Gods.

The final and most brutal edict in 304 AD forced all men, women and children to gather in designated public places to offer sacrifice to the Roman gods or face execution. However Constantius and Maximian didn't enforce this last edict in the regions under their control.

Constantine, the son of Constantius took office in July 306 AD and ended the persecution in the areas he governed and he also made restitution for the property that had been stolen from the Christians and he restored their legal status as citizens.

The persecution continued in the East, but in 307 AD the penalty for non-compliance was reduced from death to mutilation and hard labour. The mutilation involved severing the Achilles tendon of the left ankle and the blinding of the right eye according to Eusebius and hard labour usually meant working in the mines under atrocious conditions.

Galerius finally ended his eight years of terror in May 311 AD by issuing a proclamation on his death bed, but the persecution still continued in part of the East until 313 AD, when Licinius came to power.

Constantine and Licinius signed the **Edict of Milan** that year, which gave Christians and people of any other religion 'free and unrestricted opportunity to religious worship.' Constantine went on to become the sole ruler of the Roman Empire by 324 AD and he even adopted Christianity as his own religion.

Looking at the history of the church from the initial persecution by Jews of the early Christians, through to the devastation of Jerusalem and the 129 years of overall Roman persecution, it's remarkable that so much biblical material survived this period at all.

The Romans had generally been tolerant of other religions before the advent of Christianity and in fact this was part of their formula for success. They even added some foreign Gods to their own list of Gods and included them in the Pantheon, so why did they undertake these terrible persecutions against Christians?

The Roman governor Pliny wrote in around 110 AD that Christianity was 'a superstition taken to dangerous lengths.' Tacitus described it as a 'deadly superstition' and Seutonius referred to Christians as a 'class of persons given to a new and mischievous superstition.'

Some of the teachings of Christ were misunderstood by the Romans, such as the request by Jesus that believers should meet and re-enact the last supper.

The teaching that all men were equal under God, slave and free, would also have been seen as a direct threat to Roman authority, as the Empire had been built on slavery and relied on vast numbers of slaves to maintain it.

Similarly, the teaching that there was one true God and that belief in Jesus was necessary for salvation would also have been abhorrent to the Romans.

But on certain occasions it seems that emperors used Christians to divert attention from natural disasters or failings by their own administration and they were seen as a soft target. Examples of this are Nero blaming Christians for the fires of Rome and Decius blaming them for causing a famine in the country.

Apart from these reasons for persecuting Christians, we can't discount the possibility that a few of the emperors were also clinically psychopathic.

Despite the 129 years of persecution under the Romans, the original writings were carefully copied by scribes in secret so that the teachings could be distributed to the growing fellowship.

What we have today is a large number of fragments and some manuscripts of very early copies of the books comprising the Old and New Testament and these are housed in dozens of state and university libraries.

Fortunately many of the manuscripts were saved by the intervention of philanthropists such as Martin Bodmer, Chester Beatty and John Rylands.

Most scholars agree that originally there were various writing styles of the Old Testament texts in existence simultaneously. But it seems that during the period 3rd century BC to 1st century AD, the favoured version had become what is called the proto-Masoretic text and this ultimately became the template text used in the Hebrew bible.

The term Masoretic refers to a group of Hebrew scribes called the Masoretes and the name is derived from the word 'masorah' which means tradition. Their goal was to preserve the traditions of the Jewish people and so they made meticulous copies from source material, letter for letter.

Aleppo Codex

The oldest example of a complete Hebrew bible in existence is the Aleppo Codex, which was written around **930 AD** in Tiberias. This 491 page codex was written on parchment by a scribe named Shlomo Ben Boya'a, but another renowned scribe from this period named Aaron Ben Asher verified the text and he also added the Masoretic comments to the codex.

It had an intriguing history and was captured by the Crusaders in 1099 AD before being ransomed and then taken to Cairo where it was used by the Jewish philosopher Maimonides.

This rabbi, who lived from 1135 to 1204 AD, was an expert on the Torah and believed it to be the most accurate copy of the Old Testament he'd ever seen.

The codex was named after the Syrian town of Aleppo, where it remained for 572 years from 1375 AD onwards.

Unfortunately rioters burned down the Synagogue in Aleppo on 2nd December 1947, three days after the UN decision to establish a Jewish state in Palestine and only 295 of the 491 pages survived. Most of the Torah was destroyed, apart from the last few pages of Deuteronomy and the books of Esther and Daniel are also missing.

For years it was thought that the entire codex had been lost but the manuscript had actually been recovered from the flames by some brave Jews living in Aleppo. The codex was eventually smuggled out of Syria across the border into Turkey and from there it was taken to Israel in 1958 hidden inside an old washing machine!

The Aleppo Codex is regarded as the most important biblical document of the Jewish people and researchers from the Ben-Zvi Institute are still searching for the missing pages. Some historians regard its significance as being comparable to that of the English Magna Carta.

A full page was discovered in 1982 and in 2007 a fragment was found that had been carried by a man living in Brooklyn for years as a good luck charm!

Since 1993 the Aleppo codex has been housed with the Dead Sea Scrolls in the Shrine of the Book in Jerusalem.

The Masoretic text of the Hebrew bible was used as the source material for later translations into other languages and it was also used as the source text for the Old Testament books of Protestant bibles.

But apart from making copies of the Hebrew texts in Hebrew, the ancient texts were later translated into other languages such as Greek and Latin.

- Chapter 3 -
Evolution of the Bible as we know it

It's thought that in Alexandria in Egypt during the 3rd century BC that the first five books of the Old Testament (or Torah) were translated from their original Hebrew into Koine Greek.

This was probably ordered by Ptolemy II of Egypt, who ruled from 283 to 246 BC and his motivation for doing this could have been to help the large population of Jews who were living in Alexandria, who could read Greek but probably not Hebrew.

The Torah was definitely translated into Greek before 200 BC as Greek quotations from the books of Genesis and Exodus are cited in other Greek literature from before this date. Also the Greek used in the translation was early Koine, which is also called common Greek.

Koine Greek was commonly spoken in the Mediterranean region and the Middle East at that time in history and the Greek language per se was in widespread use on account of the conquests of Alexander the Great, who died in 323 BC.

Seventy, or possibly seventy-two, Jewish scribes were asked to make a Greek translation of the Hebrew Torah and this is documented in the writings of Josephus, Philo of Alexandria and also Saint Jerome.

Philo wrote that six scholars were chosen from each of the twelve tribes of Israel and on completion all the copies were thoroughly examined and found to be identical. It's believed that each scholar had to produce his own translation independently while working in complete isolation.

As seventy scribes were involved, the Greek translation is known as the **Septuagint** which means 'translation of the seventy,' but later the other books of the Hebrew Old Testament were translated and it's thought that this colossal task was finally completed by 132 BC.

So the Septuagint is the name given to the Greek translation of the books comprising the Hebrew Old Testament and this comprises thirty-nine Old Testament books as well as fourteen Apocrypha books.

The **Apocrypha** books were not translated from Hebrew source texts, because they were originally written in Greek and for this reason they were regarded as being non-canonical by some Protestant churches and the Jewish faith.

However the Eastern Orthodox Church accepted the Apocrypha books and used the Greek Septuagint as the source material for translation of the entire Old Testament in their bibles, as opposed to using the Hebrew Masoretic text.

The Catholic Church accepted the Apocrypha in its canon only after the Council of Trent in 1546 AD.

The Septuagint was later translated into Latin in a haphazard way over a period of a hundred years, but the quality of the translations varied from copy to copy as there was little co-ordination in the task of translating. These early Latin translated manuscripts of the Septuagint are called 'The Old Latin Bible' or **Vetus Latina**.

The copying of the New Testament texts by scribes would have been done in secret during the period of the Roman persecutions, but after the Edict of Milan in 313 AD the scribes could work openly.

When Christianity became the official religion of the Roman Empire it created a massive demand for copies of the texts for the new churches that were being built. What a turnaround – from 129 years of persecution to Christianity becoming the official religion of Rome!

Constantine requested Eusebius of Caesarea to provide fifty copies of the Scriptures just for the churches in Constantinople and so there are a large number of manuscripts in existence from after the Edict of Milan, but fortunately some also survived from before 313 AD.

At the Council of Rome in 382 AD, Pope Damasus and the bishops of the church agreed on a list of books that would make up the Bible for the very first time.

The pope then asked Jerome, a Catholic priest and theologian, who was also the son of Eusebius, to produce a reliable **Latin text** of the Gospels. This meant reviewing and cross referencing all the old Latin texts which had been translated from their original Greek writings and producing a single standardised Gospel text from them.

By 384 AD, Jerome had completed this translation and he'd also translated the entire Book of Psalms into Latin. But unfortunately for him, the Pope died on 11th December of that year and a few months later Jerome was forced to flee to Bethlehem because of the huge controversy that his Latin text had caused.

In Bethlehem he initially set about re-translating some Old Testament books from Greek into Latin. However he then embarked on a monumental project that took fifteen years, from 390 to 405 AD, where he converted all thirty nine books of the Hebrew bible (Old Testament) from their original Hebrew text directly into Latin.

Up until this time, all the Latin translations of the Old Testament had been made from Greek texts into Latin.

Jerome had already standardised the gospels in Latin and he may have been working on the other New Testament books as well, although this is uncertain. What is known is that other scholars were definitely involved in the translation of the balance of the New Testament into Latin. We then had for the first time in history a complete bible in Latin and this became known as the **'Vulgate.'**

Jerome is regarded as having been the second most prolific writer on Christianity from ancient times, after Augustine of Hippo, and he died in Bethlehem in 420 AD.

The Pope declared that the Vulgate was the official bible of the church and for about a thousand years, the Vulgate with its Latin text remained the official bible of the Christian churches throughout the World.

It was only in 1384 that the Vulgate was finally translated into English by John Wycliffe, John Purvey and other scholars working with them. Wycliffe was a Doctor of Divinity and Oxford University professor and was a forerunner of the Protestant reformation, who wanted the poor of England to have a bible that they could read in their own language.

It's thought that he personally translated the gospels and possibly the entire New Testament into English. However he was openly critical of many of the church teachings such as confession, transubstantiation and indulgences, which brought him into conflict with the Catholic Church.

His team produced and distributed dozens of bible manuscripts written in English but Wycliffe suffered a stroke while saying mass and died on 31st December 1384.

Thirty years later he was declared a heretic and his remains were eventually exhumed in 1428, burned and later thrown into the river Swift in Leicestershire. What's incredible is that there are still about 150 complete or incomplete manuscripts of Wycliffe's bible in existence today.

After Wycliffe's death, one of his followers, Jan Hus, continued the fight to get the Church to allow vernacular versions of the bible, which was a dangerous cause as at this time it was a capital offence to even possess a non-Latin bible!

Hus was a Czech priest and philosopher and was one of the early Church reformers, but he also voiced his criticism of Catholic Church doctrine in public and was declared a heretic.

Hus was burned at the stake in Constance in 1415 and the English translation bible manuscripts were used to start the fire at his execution.

The invention of the printing press in the 1450's gradually made the role of the scribe redundant and it's not surprising that the first book ever printed in the World was a bible in Latin.

In 1512, the Dutch priest and theologian Desiderius Erasmus began a massive project to re-translate the entire Latin New Testament. For years Erasmus had been studying the Greek New Testament manuscripts available to him, as well as several Latin Vulgate manuscripts and so he translated them in a standardised text.

Alongside the Latin wording he placed the corresponding texts in Greek and this was the first Greek New Testament ever printed (as opposed to being hand-written).

It's not entirely certain why he produced the dual texts, possibly to highlight any anomalies between the translations, but this dual translated New Testament was produced in Basel in 1516 and was an immediate success.

The name '**Textus receptus**' or received text was given to this Greek New Testament text retrospectively 120 years later. However a deficiency in the Textus receptus is that Erasmus only had access to a limited number of manuscripts.

By the end of the 1700's, as a result of comparisons to a broader range of manuscripts, these limitations became obvious and the Textus receptus was then superseded by more modern translations.

Martin Luther then translated the New Testament into German from Erasmus' Greek-Latin text and he published this version in 1522. Working alongside Luther was William Tyndale, a brilliant English bible scholar and linguist who was living in exile in Germany.

Tyndale went on to translate the New Testament into English in 1525 and he also had this version published, but in England non-Latin bibles were still being confiscated and burned and one could face execution for possessing one. This is the main reason why there are only two copies of Tyndale's first edition in existence today!

Tyndale had also written 'The Practyse of Prelates,' which opposed Henry V111's divorce on the grounds that it was against biblical teaching and so he was arrested in Brussels and then held as a prisoner in the Castle of Vilvoorde, until his execution for heresy in 1536.

Tyndale was killed by strangulation and then his body was burned at the stake, but just before his death he apparently said, "If only the King's eyes could be opened."

Another Englishman, Myles Coverdale, then translated the Old Testament into English and this meant that there was now an English translation of both the Old and New Testaments for the first time in history and so the first complete bible in English was printed in 1535.

By then a rift had developed between King Henry V111 and the Catholic Church, over the Pope's refusal to sanction his divorce from Catherine of Aragon. In response to this, Henry passed the **Supremacy Act of 1534** into law, which declared the king to be the head of the Church of England and a persecution soon broke out against the Catholic clergy and laity in England.

Although some historians have quoted the number of Catholics killed as being in the tens of thousands, it was probably more like several thousand.

Henry placed about eight hundred abbeys; monasteries, nunneries and friaries and all their lands and assets under state control. These were all dissolved, systematically being sold off, demolished or converted into other institutions between 1536 and 1540.

The vast majority of the stained glass in England was destroyed during this period and yet again a huge amount of biblical material was lost as the monastic libraries were burned to the ground.

However the new bible in English must have suited Henry's needs and so he instructed the Archbishop of Canterbury, Thomas Cranmer, to hire Myles Coverdale to print his bible.

This version, the '**Great Bible**' was distributed to all the churches in England in 1539, only three years after poor Tyndale had been executed. The king's eyes had indeed been opened!

Towards the end of his life Henry became morbidly obese and was possibly suffering from adult onset diabetes and gout, as well as having ulcerated sores on his one leg. He died aged 55 on 28th January 1547 and was succeeded by his nine year old son Edward, from his third marriage to Jane Seymour.

Edward V1 reigned for just six years until his death on 6th July 1553, but during this short period and under the advice of Thomas Cranmer, he abolished the mass and the requirement for priests to be celibate and he also mandated that all church services be said in English.

Mary, the daughter of Henry V111 and his first wife, Catherine of Aragon, reigned from July 1553 until 17th November 1558, when she died of influenza. During her five year reign she reversed many of Henry's reforms and at her first Parliament in October 1553 she declared that her parent's marriage had indeed been valid.

Mary clamped down on the possession of non-Latin bibles and clergy that had been permitted to marry after Henry's reforms, were now defrocked. She also reinstated the heresy laws at the end of 1554 and had 283 dissenters executed, nearly all burned at the stake, thereby earning herself the name 'Bloody Mary.'

Cranmer himself was burned at the stake in 1555, as well as the bishops Ridley and Latimer and the poor bible reformers again had to flee for their lives, with some going to Geneva to continue their work.

John Knox, the Protestant reformer, criticised Queen Mary and the other female monarchs in power in Europe at the time, in one of his writings, 'The first blast of the trumpet against the monstrous regiment of women,' which he wrote anonymously in Geneva in 1558.

His writings were an attack on Catholic Queens, as well as a defence of Protestantism and they soon become an impediment to him when Elizabeth became Queen the very next year. She generally supported the Protestant cause but was angered by his views on women in power.

Elizabeth 1 became Queen at the age of twenty five on 15th January 1559 and she quickly set about reversing the changes made by her half-sister Mary. Four months into her reign a new Act of Supremacy was passed and she became the 'Supreme Governor of the Church of England' and she also repealed the heresy laws.

The 'Act of Uniformity' was enacted, making it compulsory for everyone to attend Church and to use the 1552 Book of Common Prayer, although the punishment for not attending church or for failing to use the prayer book was relatively mild.

On 25th February 1570, Pope Pius issued the 'Regnans in excelsis' bull which excommunicated Elizabeth and all who obeyed her and it also mandated Catholics to rebel against her authority.

As a counter to this, Elizabeth enacted legislation in 1571 making it a treasonable offence to be a Catholic or to harbour a Catholic priest. The punishment was generally death by being hanged and then drawn and quartered, but it's unknown how many priests were executed during her reign.

Elizabeth also removed political power from Catholics by forcing all members of Parliament to swear the Oath of Supremacy, which endorsed her as Governor of the Church in England. Other institutions such as the universities of Oxford and Cambridge were also purged of all Catholics.

While they were in exile, John Calvin; Myles Coverdale; William Whittingham; John Knox; John Foxe, Anthony Gilby and others worked together on the compilation of a new bible, which came to be known as the **'Geneva Bible.'**

About 80% of the text was from Tyndale's earlier translation and all of the Old Testament was translated directly from the Hebrew texts in which they'd originally been written. Published in 1560, this was the first bible to have numbered verses and notes in the margins and it soon became highly popular.

However it had a glaring weakness, which was that some of the comments in the margins were highly inflammatory against the Catholic Church and so in 1568 a revised version was also produced, called the '**Bishops Bible**.'

During the reign of King James I, the Puritans in England began voicing their concerns about certain problems within the Church. So in January 1604 the king convened the Hampton court conference 'for the hearing and for the determining, things pretended to be amiss in the church' and this was attended by professors, bishops and other clergy.

John Reynolds, the Puritan president of Corpus Christi College, suggested that a new translation of the bible should be undertaken because of the reservations that the Puritans had with the Geneva Bible.

The King agreed and assembled forty seven of the best biblical scholars and linguists of the day to conduct this project, which took seven years to complete.

Their objective was to produce a text which was as close as possible to the original Old Testament Hebrew and New Testament Greek writings. This huge team of distinguished scholars researched all the editions of the bible previously in print and in 1611 they finally produced the **King James Bible**.

This was again heavily based on Tyndale's original work, but the researchers also used as source material various Greek translations of the New Testament as well as the Latin Vulgate.

The Old Testament was translated directly from the Hebrew texts to ensure the greatest accuracy. The King James Bible went on to become the most printed book in history!

In time biblical manuscripts were discovered which even pre-dated the source texts that had been used for the translation of the King James Bible and so in 1777, Johann Griesbach, a German biblical scholar produced a revised New Testament text. This took three years to complete and as he had access to a far wider range of manuscripts than

Erasmus had back in 1512, his text did not use Textus receptus for reference.

Thirty two years after Griesbach died, a very ancient manuscript, the **Codex Sinaiticus**, was found by chance at Saint Catherine's monastery in 1844. Westcott and Hort used this and another even older manuscript called the **Codex Vaticanus**, for the compilation of their 1881 Greek New Testament texts and they worked on this translation for some 28 years!

Since then, a wealth of ancient biblical material has been found in archaeological expeditions which has necessitated even further revisions and so the current New Testament produced by Nestle-Aland and the United Bible Societies benefit from a very diverse range of ancient source material.

The principle of basing the texts on the oldest manuscripts available and of using comparative analysis of the broadest range of texts has resulted in a very high degree of accuracy in our bibles today.

The evolution of this book is a remarkable story in human history. The Bible has its roots at the time of the Patriarchs, through to Jesus and the spread of the early church.

The events described in the Torah were first handed down by word of mouth, being carefully repeated from family to family over many generations. They then started to be written down on parchment scrolls and on papyrus without the writings being formalised into consistent texts.

Then the trauma of slavery and the loss of their country and their temple forced the Israelites to standardise the writings, so that they could preserve their heritage for future generations. The texts were then diligently copied, letter by letter at the hands of many generations of Jewish scribes.

There were universal persecutions of Christians totalling 129 years under various Emperors which killed many thousands of people, destroyed a great number of churches and resulted in a huge quantity of biblical manuscripts being lost.

Then there was the persecution during the Reformation and the mass burning of bibles and yet somehow the texts survived through to this day.

Probably the greatest destroyer of texts was nature herself, through water damage; ultraviolet light degradation; oxidation, moulds and even insect pests.

Many reformers lost their lives for making translations into the vernacular, but their work was not in vain and these translations and the invention of the printing press brought accessibility of the Bible to the masses for the first time in history.

Then there were the twists of fate, such as the discovery of Codex Sinaiticus, an ancient manuscript found in a waste paper basket at St Catherine's monastery by Tischendorf.

Later in 1946/1947 the Dead Sea Scrolls were discovered, which rocked the world of archaeology, as this treasure trove of biblical and historical texts had been left undisturbed in caves since 68 AD!

Today we benefit from translations of texts from the widest range of ancient source material, that have undergone the greatest scrutiny imaginable and so they should be regarded as being highly reliable.

- Chapter 4 -
Ancient source texts of the Bible

So the text of the bibles we read today have been taken from ancient source texts, but where are these source manuscripts today?

To date no autographed original books of the Old or New Testament have been found, which given their age is to be expected. Unfortunately it wasn't the custom for scribes to date their work and the oldest dated manuscripts that have been found are the Uspenski gospels which were written in Greek in 835 AD.

What we do have are a few virtually complete copies of the Old and New Testament from the fourth century, one of which is dated to as early as 325 AD.

In addition to this there are thousands of pages, part pages and fragments from very early copies of these books, with some Old Testament texts dating back to the 1st and 2nd centuries BC!

The oldest complete manuscript of the entire Bible yet found is the **Codex Amiatinus**, which is a Latin Vulgate edition and was written around 716 AD at the monasteries of Monkwearmouth and Jarrow in Northumbria.

Codex Amiatinus was named after the place where it was found, the Abbazia di San Salvatore on Mount Amiata in Tuscany.

St Peter's Monkwearmouth was founded by Benedict in 674 AD and he founded Jarrow eight years later, which is where the Venerable Bede had his early education and as the monasteries were only eleven kilometres apart they functioned as one. This bible is now kept at the Biblioteca Medicea Laurenziana in Florence.

There are also three virtually complete parchment manuscripts of the entire bible written in Greek. Two of these, the Codex Vaticanus and the Codex Sinaiticus are dated to the early to mid 4th century.

The third is the Codex Alexandrinus, which is dated between the late 4th and the early 5th century.

Codex Vaticanus

This codex is dated to around 325 AD and is thought to be the oldest copy of a virtually complete bible in existence.

There's been much debate about whether it was written in Rome, Egypt or Asia Minor and the codex comprises 759 original pages, 617 from the Old Testament and 142 from the New Testament.

It's clear that several scribes worked on this manuscript which is made of calf skin and all the text is in uncials and has none of the text modifications that are found in the later manuscripts.

Uncials are rounded capital letters that were used by Greek and Latin scribes especially from the 4th to the 8th century.

The original Old Testament texts missing from the codex were a large part of Genesis and also part of Psalm 105 and the New Testament texts missing are Paul's letters to Timothy; Titus, Philemon and part of Hebrews as well as the book of Revelation.

However at some later date the texts missing from the original codex were added and this may have been done shortly before the codex was presented to the Vatican after the Council of Florence (1438-1445).

It's thought that Vaticanus was in Constantinople before being taken to the Vatican but it was definitely in the Vatican library by 1475 as it was listed in the catalogue of that year.

Even Napoleon Bonaparte was fascinated by this codex and he took it to Paris in 1809, but fortunately he returned it to the Holy See 6 years later in 1815.

Vaticanus is of immense significance due to its age and was the main source material used by Westcott and Hort in their edition of 'The New Testament in the original Greek' in 1881.

Most of the commonly sold editions of the New Testament are largely based on Vaticanus and it is still stored at the Biblioteca Apostolica in the Vatican to this day.

Codex Sinaiticus

This manuscript is thought to have been written around 350 AD and was discovered in the library of St Catherine's Greek Orthodox monastery at the base of Mount Sinai - the mountain mentioned in Exodus where Moses received the Ten Commandments. St Catherine's monastery claims to be the oldest inhabited Christian monastery in the World and was built around 565 AD.

The codex was discovered by the German theologian Constantine von Tischendorf, who was on a mission to find ancient biblical manuscripts, hopefully older than the source material that had been used for the Textus receptus text.

His search had taken him to dozens of libraries, monasteries and convents in Europe and the Middle East, but his research eventually led him to St Catherine's in the May of 1844. It was here that Tischendorf made the discovery that he described as being the pearl of all his researches!

He was studying old manuscripts in the library when he noticed a large waste paper basket which contained parchments of the Old Testament that were written in Greek. The manuscripts aroused his curiosity because they looked extremely old and so he asked the librarian about them. The librarian said that he intended to burn them and that he'd already burned two similar piles of old manuscripts, which he thought were of no importance whatsoever!

Tischendorf was allowed to take 43 of the parchment pages back to Saxony, but by then he'd accumulated debts and to cover these he was forced to sell fifty other manuscripts gathered on his expeditions, to the University of Leipzig.

The monks at Saint Catherine's later realised the value of the parchments and wouldn't release the remaining 86 pages, so Tischendorf returned in February 1853 in order to copy the ancient texts letter by letter.

Now on this visit he found another page of the codex containing eleven lines of Genesis, which indicated to him that the codex may have originally been a complete copy of the entire Old Testament.

In January 1859 he returned for a third time and made a very significant discovery, again purely by chance. One night the steward of the convent was chatting to Tischendorf and during the conversation mentioned that for years he'd kept one old manuscript in his room, instead of in the library itself. He asked the steward if he could inspect it and to his complete amazement found that it contained part of the Old Testament and the **entire New Testament** written in Greek.

Tischendorf later wrote, 'I knew that I held in my hand the most precious Bible treasure in existence – a document whose age and importance exceeded that of all the manuscripts which I had ever examined during twenty years study of the subject.'

Tischendorf was allowed to borrow the codex and he took it to St Petersburg where he spent three years transcribing the entire manuscript. He then presented it to the Emperor of Russia in October 1862, perhaps because the Emperor had funded his entire third trip!

In March 1865, Tischendorf was made an Honorary Doctor by both Cambridge and Oxford Universities in recognition for his work and for making 'the find of the century.'

Codex Sinaiticus contains much of the Old Testament and is the oldest complete copy of the New Testament yet discovered. The greater part of the codex (347 pages) was sold to the British museum by the Russian government in 1933 for £100,000. Today Codex Sinaiticus can be found at the Sir John Ritblat Gallery, which is in the British Library in St Pancras, London.

Forty three pages are held at the University Library in Leipzig and parts of six pages are at the National Library of Russia in St Petersburg, with the remaining eighteen pages still at St Catherine's Monastery! This parchment codex is also dated by palaeographical analysis to the middle of the 4th century AD.

It's quite possible that Vaticanus and Sinaiticus were located together in Caesarea at one time, as both codices use the same system to divide the book of Acts into 36 chapters.

Although Sinaiticus is extremely old, it's generally accepted that Vaticanus is even older and so the text of the Gospels in most editions of the New Testament today are closer to Vaticanus than they are to Sinaiticus.

Codex Alexandrinus

This ancient manuscript is believed to have been written in Egypt in the late 4th or early 5th century and so it's more recent than Vaticanus and Sinaiticus. It's made of Vellum and consists of 630 pages of the Old Testament and 143 pages of the New Testament written in Greek.

It was originally one volume but is now bound as four small volumes, three of the Old Testament and one of the New Testament and only ten pages of the Old Testament and thirty one pages of the New Testament have been lost. It's also the earliest codex discovered to have had titles for the major chapters.

Alexandrinus was originally at the Patriarchal library in Alexandria, but in 1621 it was taken to Constantinople by Cyril Lucar, the Patriarch of Alexandria.

He later sent it as a gift to King James 1 of England, who unfortunately died just before he was able to receive it. However, Charles 1 later accepted the gift in 1627 and it was then donated to the British library in St Pancras, where it's still on display to this day.

Vaticanus and Alexandrinus are the oldest surviving almost complete manuscripts of the Old Testament in Greek and by comparison the oldest complete Old Testament manuscript in Hebrew is from the mid 10th century AD.

Vaticanus, Sinaiticus and Alexandrinus are Septuagint manuscripts in Greek, but there are also some ancient manuscripts of the Latin Vulgate such as **Codex Fuldensis**, which is dated to around 545 AD.

In addition to these virtually complete manuscripts, thousands of fragments of ancient texts have been discovered, many of which are considerably older than Vaticanus.

For example, fragments of texts of Leviticus and Deuteronomy from as far back as the 2nd century BC have been found as well as fragments from the first century BC of Genesis; Exodus; Leviticus, Numbers and Deuteronomy.

A collection of papyrus documents now referred to as the **Oxyrhynchus papyri**, were discovered at the site of the ancient settlement of Oxyrhynchus, which is 160 km South of Cairo. The town of Oxyrhynchus was the centre of Christianity in Egypt in the 4th and 5th centuries.

The papyri were uncovered in five expeditions between 1896 and 1934 by two archaeologists, Hunt and Grenfell, who found thousands of ancient documents, including some biblical papyrus and vellum manuscripts.

Incredibly, many of the finds were discovered at a waste dumping ground outside the town! This find was hugely significant and as at 2015, of the 131 New Testament papyri that had been discovered worldwide, 47 are thought to have come from Oxyrhynchus.

A system for classifying these ancient specimens, which are often just fragments of text, was produced by Alfred Rahlfs in 1914. Rahlfs was a German Professor of the Old Testament who did extensive research on the Septuagint from 1907 to 1933.

They're also classified under the Gregory-Aland system which was used by Caspar Gregory as far back as 1908.

Papyri are designated 'P' followed by a number and those found at Oxyrhynchus are denoted P.Oxy followed by a number allocated to each papyrus fragment.

Some pages and fragments were also allocated a code relating to the philanthropist who originally acquired them, so there will be more than one reference number for a given piece of ancient text and a few interesting examples are described below.

The Swiss Philanthropist **Martin Bodmer** (1899-1971) purchased **P66**, which contains 92% of the gospel of John written in Greek and which is dated to around **200 AD**, making it one of the oldest New Testament manuscripts ever found. It was found near Dishna in Egypt in 1952 and the 75 page codex is in remarkably good condition. An example of the text is that of John 1:3:

'All things came into being through him; and apart from him not one thing came into being which had come into being.'

Today the codex is stored at the library he founded, the Bodmeriana Library in Cologny, Switzerland.

Another Bodmer papyrus is **P75**, dated to between **175 and 225 AD**, which was found at Pabau in Egypt and is now in the Vatican library. It contains half of the gospels of Luke and John written in Greek and 102 pages have survived from an original codex of 144 pages.

Chester Beatty (1875–1968), the Irish-American mining magnate, was another great philanthropist who had an interest in ancient biblical texts and he purchased eleven papyrus manuscripts, nine of which were dated to either the second or third centuries AD and are thus even older than Vaticanus!

These are of great value to biblical historians because they were written before the final and bloody persecution of Christians which began on 24th February 303 AD. Vaticanus and Sinaiticus were both written after the purge had ended.

This ten year purge by Galerius and the Tetrarchy mandated the burning of all Christian writings throughout the empire, so it's quite remarkable that they survived the purge never mind surviving to the present day.

The Chester Beatty manuscripts were purchased from an antiquities dealer and it's thought that they were originally found close to Fayum or Aphroditopolus in Egypt, possibly in clay jars in a Coptic (Christian Egyptian) graveyard.

P45 or Chester Beatty I was copied in Greek around **250 AD** and so is one of the oldest New Testament writings in existence. The codex originally contained the four Gospels and Acts written on 220 pages, but only 30 have survived. It contains 2 pages of Matthew's gospel; 6 pages of Mark; 7 from Luke, 2 of John as well as 13 pages of Acts and it can be found at the Chester Beatty Library in Dublin Castle.

One page contains Matthew 25:41 to 26:39 and this particular specimen can be found at the Austrian National Library in Vienna.

Then he will say to those on his left, "Depart from me you who are cursed, into the eternal fire prepared for the devil and his angels. For I was hungry and you gave me nothing to eat, I was thirsty and you gave me nothing to drink, I was a stranger and you did not invite me in. I needed clothes and you did not clothe me, I was sick and in prison and you did not look after me…"

P46 or Chester Beatty II is a papyrus codex of 86 pages out of an original 104 and it contains the last eight chapters of Romans and almost all of Corinthians. It also has all of Paul's letters to the

Hebrews; Ephesians; Galatians, Philippians and the Colossians as well as two chapters of 1 Thessalonians.

It's not known where the manuscript was found but it was probably Cairo and the antiquities dealer unfortunately separated the pages of the codex before selling them, presumably to try and get a better price.

Chester Beatty bought 10 pages in 1930 and another 46 in 1935 and the University of Michigan bought 6 pages in 1931 and a further 24 in 1933, but the whereabouts of the missing 18 pages remains a mystery!

There's controversy over the age of P46 but the most likely date range is **175 to 225 AD**. Some of the codex is housed at the Chester Beatty Library in Dublin and some at the University of Michigan.

Another very old specimen is **Chester Beatty VI**, which comprises portions of 50 pages out of an original codex of 108 of the books of Numbers and Deuteronomy. This is dated to around **150 AD** and is believed to be the oldest codex ever found that is written on papyrus as opposed to parchment. The codex is housed at the Chester Beatty library except for a few fragments which are now at the University of Michigan.

Another great philanthropist was **John Rylands** (1801-1888), an English businessman who made a fortune in the textiles industry. He funded orphanages and old age homes and had special editions of the bible printed, which he distributed to the poor for free.

The John Rylands library houses some extremely old papyrus specimens including P457, the oldest piece of New Testament scripture yet found and P458, the oldest specimen of the Septuagint discovered thus far.

Probably the oldest piece of New Testament scripture ever found is the **St John's fragment**, which is a tiny section of a papyrus codex of the gospel of John, designated **Rylands Papyrus 457** (or P52). There's also controversy over it's age but it was originally dated in terms of paleography to between **100 and 150 AD** and more recently to between 125 and 175 AD.

This is absolutely remarkable when it's considered that John is believed to have written his gospel around 90 AD in Ephesus. So in a very short time after John wrote his gospel, copies of his writings had already made their way to Egypt!

It must originally have been from a codex as the fragment is written on both sides with John 18:31-33 on the one side and John 18:37-38 on the other. There are only 114 legible letters, but had the missing letters been preserved, when translated into English, it would have read:

the Jews, "For us it is not permitted to kill anyone," so that the word of Jesus might be fulfilled, which he spoke signifying what kind of death he was going to die. Entered therefore again into the Praetorium Pilate and summoned Jesus and said to him, "Thou art king of the Jews?"

… a King I am. For this I have been born and for this I have come into the world so that I would testify to the truth. Everyone who is of the truth hears of me my voice. Said to him Pilate, "What is truth?" and this having said, again he went out unto the Jews and said to them, "I find not one fault in him."

The fragments comprising P457 were with some papyri purchased by Bernard Grenfell in Egypt in 1920 and this fragment is now part of a collection of thousands of fragments and documents discovered in North Africa and Greece.

Rylands Papyrus 458 (also designated Rahlfs 957) consists of 8 tiny fragments of a papyrus scroll of Deuteronomy (25:1-3) written in Greek and is dated to the **mid 2nd century BC**, making it the oldest writing of the Septuagint in existence! It's thought that the fragments were found in the cartonnage of a mummy at Fayum in Egypt that was purchased by Dr Rendel Harris in 1917.

What's believed to be the second oldest surviving specimen of the Septuagint is **Papyrus Fouad 266** which was found at Fayum in 1939. 117 fragments of this scroll have survived with writings from Deuteronomy and it's generally dated to the **1st century BC** although some date it to the 2nd century BC.

Fayum was founded in 4000 BC and is the oldest town in Egypt. Today the papyri are at the Egyptian Papyrological society in Cairo.

P104 is a fragment of a papyrus codex dated to the **late second century** written in Greek and it contains parts of six verses from the gospel of Matthew, including the Parable of the Tenants. The fragment is one of the oldest copies of the writings of Matthew and was also found at Oxyrhynchus. Today it is at the Sackler Library in Oxford.

P87 is a fragment of a copy of St Paul's letter to Philemon and was written in Greek on Papyrus and is dated to about **250 AD**. St Paul wrote this letter around 60-61 AD while he was in prison, but it's not certain where the fragment was found. It's now housed at the Institute Fur Altertumskunde at Koln University.

The **Magdalen Papyrus** (P64) is another fascinating example of an ancient biblical text and it's been the subject of much debate regarding its age. It was purchased in Luxor, Egypt in 1901 by Charles Huleatt and consists of three fragments with words from the gospel of Matthew written in Greek. As the fragments were written on both sides of the papyrus, they would have been part of a codex as opposed to a scroll.

The specimens were dated to around **200 AD** by four leading papyrologists (Roberts; Bell, Skeat and Turner), but in 1994 Carsten Thiede proposed a date as early as the middle of the first century. Two other experts in this field, Philip Comfort and David Barret, dated the fragments to between 150 and 175 AD. Today the specimens are housed at Magdalen College in Oxford University.

The papyrus **P90** is dated to about **175 AD** and contains text from John 18:36 through to 19:7 and the Greek writing is on both sides of the page, which is unfortunately in poor condition. Below is the translation in English of the complete text of John 19:1-7, although in the papyrus some of the letters or words were missing.

> scourged him. And the soldiers having woven a crown of thorns, they put it on his head, and a robe of purple they put around him, and they did come to him, and they said "Hail, King of the Jews!" and they gave him blows with their hands. And went forth again Pilate, and said unto them, "Behold, I bring him to you forth, so that you may know that fault in him I do not find." Came forth then Jesus without, wearing the crown of thorns, and the purple robe. And Pilate saith unto them, "Behold the man!" When they so saw him, the chief priests and officers cried out, saying, "Crucify him!" Saith unto them Pilate, "Take ye him, and crucify him: for I do not find in him guilt. Answered the Jews, "We have a law, and according to that …

This remarkable papyrus was discovered at Oxyrhynchus and is now part of the collection of the Sackler Library in Oxford.

- Chapter 5 -
Dead Sea scrolls

Sometime between November 1946 and January 1947, seven scrolls in clay pots were accidentally found by a Bedouin shepherd named Muhammed edh-Dhib, his cousin and a friend in a cave at Khirbet Qumran.

The sixteen year old Muhammed had been throwing stones into some of the dozens of small limestone caves in the area when he was surprised to hear the sound of breaking pottery in one of them. This aroused his curiosity and so he climbed down into the cave, where he discovered the scrolls that were inside several clay pots. The site is roughly a mile inland on the northwest shore of the Dead Sea in the present day West Bank, 13 miles east of Jerusalem.

One of the scrolls the young Muhammed picked up that day would prove to be of immense significance to the world of archaeology and would come to be known as the **Isaiah Scroll**. It's undoubtedly one of the most important archaeological discoveries in history.

The shepherds had no idea of the value of the scrolls they held in their hands but took them to an antiquities dealer in Bethlehem anyway. He told them that they were worthless, possibly because he suspected that they may have been stolen from a synagogue and didn't want to get involved.

They then took the scrolls to a part-time antiques dealer and cobbler named Kando in a market near Jerusalem, leaving one scroll with him and selling three of the other scrolls to another dealer for just £7.

The scrolls were sold on, but ultimately three of the scrolls were purchased for the Hebrew University of Jerusalem by Eleazar Sukenik, a professor in archaeology, from another antiquities dealer in Bethlehem.

It was Sukenik who later proposed the idea that the scrolls may have been linked to an Essene community who had been living at Qumran. Mar Samuel of the Syrian Orthodox Monastery of St Mark in Jerusalem, bought the other four scrolls and then took them over to the United States.

Dr John Trever who worked for the American Schools of Oriental Research, examined the scrolls and soon realised their importance, because the writings were similar to that of the ancient **Nash Papyrus**. At that time this papyrus was the oldest known biblical manuscript in the World, dating back to around **100-150 BC**.

The Nash Papyrus had been purchased by Dr Walter Nash from an antiquities dealer in 1902 and is just four fragments of a single sheet of papyrus with writings in Hebrew. The writings were the Ten Commandments but also the beginning of the Shema Yisrael prayer which devout Jews used to recite. The Nash papyrus is thought to have originated at Fayum in Egypt and is now at the Cambridge University library.

So about one year after the discovery by the Bedouin, a systematic search of the area began in an attempt to find the original cave, but it was only finally located in January 1949, about two years after the initial discovery.

From then until 1956 there were various archaeological expeditions involving about forty of the caves, but the Bedouin were also actively searching the area. In fact the Bedouin proved remarkably successful, because of the eleven caves containing manuscripts that were discovered, six were found by archaeologists and five by them!

Although most of the manuscripts were found in just eleven caves, about 90% of the material was found in one particular cave, designated cave four. Several more scrolls were eventually discovered in these limestone caves as well as thousands of fragments of other manuscripts, most of which were dated in the range **225 BC to 68 AD**.

About 85% of the manuscripts were made of parchment, with the rest being written on papyrus, apart from one interesting text that had been inscribed on copper. Although most of the writings were in Hebrew, there were many texts in Aramaic and a few writings in Greek.

The four scrolls that had been taken to the United States were later bought by Yigael Yadin, the son of Eleazar Sukenik in 1954 who then took them back to Israel. Yadin was himself a prominent archaeologist but he'd also once held the post of Chief of Staff of the Israeli military.

It's thought that a community of monastic farmers lived in the valley at Qumran from around 130 BC onwards and the community was probably made up of celibate men who were preparing themselves for what they perceived to be the end of the old world and the beginning of a new world order.

The community had extremely strict rules and they maintained extensive archives of all the Old Testament writings. They're thought to have fled the settlement around 68 AD in the middle of the Jewish Roman war to escape the legions of Vespasian and his son Titus.

Many of the manuscripts had carefully been placed in clay jars and then covered, but others had just been dumped on the ground in piles, possibly in their haste to escape the Roman army.

Unfortunately the manuscripts that were left unprotected disintegrated over time into many thousands of tiny fragments. These documents are some of the oldest surviving biblical writings in existence as they all pre-date 68 AD, with some having been written as far back as the third century BC.

In order to date ancient manuscripts like these, paleographers have to compare the writing styles used with other manuscripts where the date has been established and they also use references to historical events in the text, where the date of the event is definitive.

Scanning laser microscopes are sometimes used to determine the thickness of the papyrus and to identify minute characteristics of the writing, whereas radiocarbon dating can be used to give a date range of the larger manuscripts, although this is not practical on small fragments.

Some of the scrolls had been wrapped in linen to protect them and Carbon 14 dating of the linen was undertaken and later some of the scrolls themselves were carbon dated, with one test giving a date range of 385 BC to 82 AD.

The age of the find has been corroborated by other evidence such as the discovery in a cave in 1955 of three ceramic pots which contained 561 silver coins dated from 135 BC onwards.

Further evidence comes from the paleographic comparison of the manuscripts, which also generally dates the material in the range 225 BC to 50 AD.

The **Isaiah Scroll** is regarded as being one of the greatest finds and it's a virtually complete parchment scroll of the book of Isaiah written in Hebrew. All 66 chapters of Isaiah are represented in this enormous scroll which is 7.3 metres long and 0.3 metres high. The Isaiah Scroll is also in the best condition of all of the manuscripts of the Hebrew Bible or Tanakh that were found at Qumran.

Pieces of the scroll have been Carbon 14 dated several times, with one range given of 202-107 BC. Paleographic dating places it in the 150-100 BC range and so a date is often quoted for the Isaiah Scroll of around **125 BC**.

When it was found in late 1946, the Isaiah Scroll was about 1050 years older than the oldest manuscript of the Hebrew bible known to exist, which was the Aleppo Codex.

The significance of this was monumental as it allowed a direct comparison to be made of the ancient Hebrew texts of Isaiah from Qumran from 125 BC, with the Masoretic texts of Isaiah in the Aleppo Codex from 930 AD.

In the caves another twenty manuscripts of the Book of Isaiah were found and in cave two there were about one hundred fragments of the Torah; Jeremiah; Job, Psalms and Ruth, but for some reason no fragments of Genesis were found in this cave.

Cave four, which was a hand cut cave, contained about 15,000 fragments from a few hundred scrolls representing the entire Old Testament with the exception of the book of Esther. Also found here was a fragment of the book of Samuel which is possibly as old as the **3rd century BC** and so this may be the oldest biblical writing ever to have been discovered.

Of the material that could be identified, about 40% comprised writings from the Hebrew Bible, but much of the material was non-biblical and related to various aspects of life in the commune and the community rules. Examples of these are the manual of discipline and the War Scroll, which was one of the original seven scrolls found.

One of the non-biblical finds from cave three was a scroll made from two rolls of copper which listed the location of 64 underground sites of hidden gold and silver. The precious metals were possibly moved out of the temple in Jerusalem during the Jewish Roman war to prevent it falling into Roman hands. The Copper was highly oxidised and couldn't be unrolled without damaging it, but after some debate it was decided to carefully cut the scroll into 23 strips in order to decipher the Hebrew text.

There's controversy over the age of the scroll but it's generally dated to around 50 AD and to date the locations of the buried silver and gold have yet to be identified! The Copper Scroll can be found at the Jordan Archaeological Museum in Amman.

Some of the fragments from Qumran written in Greek are extremely old, such as **Rahlfs 819** which is one of the oldest Septuagint writings ever found. This is a fragment from a parchment roll with writings from Deuteronomy 11 and is dated to the **1st or 2nd century BC**.

The papyrus fragment **Rahlfs 805** also has writings from Exodus and is probably a little younger but still from the **1st or 2nd century BC**.

So Rahlfs 819 and 805 found in cave 4 at Qumran are only slightly younger than Rylands Papyrus 458 and Papyrus Fouad 266 that were discovered in Egypt.

These specimens are the four oldest surviving texts of the Hebrew bible written in Greek (Septuagint) in existence. Of course at Qumran, texts even older than these were found, but these were written in ancient Hebrew as opposed to the Greek language.

However even the oldest manuscripts and scrolls found at Qumran dating back as far as the 2nd century BC, are all still **copies of texts** and not the original texts themselves.

Due to the massive number of documents found, it's clear that the scribes at Qumran had been copying the biblical texts over a period of several decades and they must have maintained very extensive archives. Since 1967 the Isaiah scroll and the other Dead Sea scrolls have been housed at 'the Shrine of the Book' in Jerusalem.

So far we've discussed where the ancient texts comprising the Bible were discovered and where these texts can be found today and we've also looked at how the Bible evolved into its current form.

But is it possible that the scribes regularly made mistakes while making copies of the original texts? Clearly this is important, as our modern Bibles are derived from source texts copied over many centuries.

The concept of making exact replicas of existing texts down to the letter may seem strange today, but this was how the Jewish scribes worked, as they believed that the word of God was sacred and not a letter could be changed.

Jesus himself was acutely aware of the importance of individual letters in the sacred texts.

Matthew 5:18: "I tell you the truth, until heaven and earth disappear, not the smallest letter, not the least stroke of a pen, will by any means disappear from the Law until everything is accomplished."

To show the care taken in making a copy of a text we can look at the methodology of the Masoretes, who were a group of Jews who produced hand written copies of biblical texts in Hebrew for hundreds of years. The texts they produced were all in capital letters and they lacked any punctuation or paragraphs.

In the page margins of the manuscripts were notes called 'Masorah parva' which gave the exact number of letters on the page and other information and these were used as reference points by the copyists to ensure accuracy. So after copying each page of text, the number of letters in the copied page could be counted and checked against the template document.

The scribes were not permitted to copy sentence for sentence or word for word, but they had to copy letter for letter. Other scribes would sum total the letters on the copied page and check the middle letter to that of the original.

If it differed, then the page was discarded and the scribe would have to start again. The same was done to pinpoint the middle of the entire copied manuscript on its completion and a single error would result in that manuscript being destroyed so that it could never be used itself as a template for further copies.

All the copies of the Hebrew text produced by the Masoretes over the centuries are incredibly consistent and this shows the great care taken by these scribes to get their texts letter perfect.

A major study was undertaken to compare the text of the first and second century BC Isaiah scrolls found at Qumran, with the 10th century AD Masoretic Hebrew text of the Aleppo Codex.

Millar Burrows (1899-1990) who became Professor Emeritus at Yale Divinity School was involved in this extensive research and after completing his detailed analysis of the two texts, he wrote:

'It is a matter of wonder that through something like one thousand years the text went through so little alteration.'

Another world-renowned researcher in the field of paleography, Sir **Fredrick Kenyon** (1863-1952) who was also Director of the British Museum, concluded after his research:

'The last foundation for any doubt that the scriptures have come down to us substantially as they have been written, has been removed. The Christian can take the whole Bible in his hand without fear or hesitation that he holds in it the true Word of God, handed down without essential loss from generation to generation throughout the centuries.'

Gleason Archer (1916-2004) also researched the two texts. He was Professor of the Old Testament at Trinity Evangelical Divinity School in Illinois from 1965 to 1986 and he was also part of the team that translated the NIV Bible, which was published in 1978.

Archer concluded that the texts were word for word identical with the standard Hebrew Bible in more than 95% of the text and that the 5% differences were mainly minor spelling differences.

For example a comparison of the whole of Isaiah 53 (a prophecy of the death of the Messiah) found at Qumran with the Masoretic text reveals that only one word differs and this word does not change the meaning of the passage in any way.

This is utterly incredible as there are over one thousand years of history and copying copies of copies between the time of the Isaiah scroll and that of the 10th century Aleppo codex!

No **New Testament** manuscripts were found at Qumran which is to be expected, as the earliest writings of the New Testament are believed to be Paul's first letter to the Thessalonians and his letter to the Galatians from around 48-52 AD.

There's been tremendous debate over whether the gospel of Matthew or that of Mark was the first to be written and it's generally thought that both were completed before 70 AD.

One of the reasons for believing this is that the two Drachma Temple tax was mentioned in Matthew 17:24. The Temple was destroyed by the Romans in 70 AD when revenue-raising for the Temple would clearly have ceased.

So given the time of writing of the New Testament and the fact that the Essene community lived in isolation and that they'd left by around 68 AD, it's not surprising that no New Testament writings were found there.

One wonders what St Paul meant when he referred to 'treasure in jars of clay' in his second letter to the Corinthians. Paul had studied under the Pharisee Gamaliel, who was a Doctor of Law and also President of the Great Sanhedrin in Jerusalem and being very well educated he would have been aware of the community at Qumran and possibly the activities of their scribes. After all the community had been living at Qumran for several generations.

Paul wrote in 2 Corinthians 4:7:

'But we have this treasure in jars of clay to show that this all-surpassing power is from God and not from us.'

- Chapter 6 -
Historical setting at the time of Jesus

According to biblical writings, Jesus was born in Bethlehem in Judea and the town is estimated to have had a population of between 300 and 1000 inhabitants at the time.

The Jewish nation was living under Roman rule but was permitted freedom of worship, freedom to conduct the requirements of Judaic Law and they were also allowed to trade and to travel. However there were restrictions placed on them, so for example they weren't allowed to produce their own currency.

Tensions certainly existed, especially over the issue of taxation and on a few occasions this flared up into open rebellion which was met with violent suppression.

Some of the uprisings had started off as small, localised events but had rapidly gathered momentum and the most famous of these was the uprising by Spartacus and 70 other gladiators in 73 BC.

This small group escaped from the gladiatorial training school at Capua and in a short period of time managed to attract a following of 70,000 men. Spartacus and his army won some notable victories against the Romans, including the defeat of two whole legions comprising about 10,000 men.

Even when the Roman general Marcus Licinius Crassus was given overall command of a standing army of 40,000 crack legionaries to subdue the rebellion, it took several battles and very high casualties to finally defeat Spartacus in 71 BC.

It's interesting that although Spartacus is believed to have died in his final battle near present day Strongoli in Calabria, his body was never found.

Augustus Caesar was the ruler of the Empire at the time of Jesus' birth, but each of the provinces was administered by a regional governor or procurator.

The Jewish ruler at the time of the birth of Jesus was Herod the Great, who was in fact not a full blooded Jew at all and who had been appointed by Augustus. Herod was deeply unpopular with the majority of the Jews because of his punitive taxation policies and the historian Josephus mentioned this in his work **'The Jewish Antiquities'** written around 93 AD:

'Since he spent far beyond his means, Herod was obliged to show himself more severe towards his subjects by imposing heavy taxes.'

The Sadducees were in the minority numerically but they had historically enjoyed disproportionate power in Jewish society as they were at the centre of the aristocracy and they had controlled the Sanhedrin.

Their teachings were totally at odds with the Pharisees, as the Sadducees didn't believe that man had a spirit or that angels existed or even that there was a life after death.

Herod was also hated by most Sadducees because he'd systematically dismantled the power base of the old ruling dynasty, the Hasmonean Royal House and many Sadducees were members of this dynasty which had ruled from 140 BC.

Herod did this by cleverly marrying into the Hasmonean line and then by appointing his own father-in-law as the high priest. He also had 45 senior ranking Sadducees executed, restricted the jurisdiction of the Sanhedrin to purely doctrinal law and granted himself power to appoint all future presidents of the counsel.

He had also angered Jews from all sects by installing the symbol of Roman power, an Eagle, at the entrance to the Temple of Jerusalem.

In the last few years of his life, Herod seems to have become increasingly paranoid and unpredictable and he had two of his own sons killed by strangulation in 7 BC and he also executed three hundred of his military leaders.

That same year, he killed a group of influential Pharisees who had made a prophecy to his wife that he would ultimately lose his throne and that it would be lost to his descendants forever.

Apart from the biblical account of the slaughter of the Holy Innocents which he ordered, the final act of brutality that we know of happened a few days before his own death, when Herod had his third son murdered.

After Herod the Great died, his surviving son Herod Antipas became Tetrarch of the provinces of Galilee and Peraea and it was Antipas that years later ordered the beheading of John the Baptist and who questioned and mocked Jesus before sending him back to Pilate during his trial.

The Roman Emperor who ruled for much of Jesus' life was Tiberius (14-37 AD) but there was also a Roman governor of Judea and the governor at the time of the death of Jesus was Pontius Pilate.

Pilate had a history of dealing harshly with the Jews and had been reprimanded over this by Tiberius on at least two occasions. There were simmering tensions and it's interesting that it was fear of an uprising that ultimately persuaded Pilate to pass the death penalty on Jesus.

The centre of Jewish life was the Temple of Jerusalem and their religious rulers were held in very high regard by the people. The High Priest at the time of the trial of Jesus was Caiaphas, but his father-in-law Annas seems to have exerted considerable power behind the scenes.

After all Annas had himself been High Priest as had five of his sons in succession before Caiaphas and it's thought that Annas even had apartments within the residence of Caiaphas in Jerusalem.

In each town there was a court named a Sanhedrin made up of twenty three judges, but appeals and serious cases were heard at the Great Sanhedrin in Jerusalem, which was analogous to today's High Court.

This was usually led by the High Priest and a vice Chief Justice and there were sixty nine general members. The court had powers to enact many forms of justice, with the Sanhedrin convening every day of the year except on Sabbaths and during religious festivals.

Apart from the friction between the Jews and the Romans, there was also enmity between Jews and Samaritans and this was firmly rooted in ancient history.

After King Solomon had died in 931 BC, the nation had split into a southern kingdom of Judah and a northern kingdom of Israel, with the city of Samaria being established as the capital of Israel and Jerusalem the capital of Judah.

In 726 BC, Shalmaneser V, the King of Assyria, invaded Israel and besieged the city of Samaria and after a war lasting three years routed the Israelites and took most of the population into captivity.

The people left behind in Israel were predominantly farmers, as the artisans and intellectuals had been taken into Assyrian held territories and over time they married people from Syria and Mesopotamia who came to settle in Israel.

They also took on some of their customs and religious practices and the leaders of the southern kingdom, which comprised the tribes of Judah and Benjamin, were highly critical of this inter-marrying and the forsaking of some of their ancient traditions.

Later, in 586 BC, Judah itself was invaded and the Babylonians destroyed the city of Jerusalem and its temple and the majority of the citizens of Judah were themselves taken into captivity.

They remained in captivity for 47 years until the fall of the Babylonian Empire in 539 BC, when Cyrus the Great of Persia permitted them to return to Jerusalem and it's no coincidence that construction of the second temple began the very next year in 538 BC.

Now the Samaritans openly welcomed their ancestral brothers when they returned from exile and were eager to participate in the construction of the second temple, but their offer was flatly refused.

Of course this rejection by Judah in not allowing Samaritans to participate in the construction of their temple, further fuelled anger between the two peoples. Including periods of inactivity, the second Temple of Jerusalem took about twenty three years to build and was finally completed in 515 BC.

The Samaritans later built their own temple on Mount Gerizim, which they regarded as being their most sacred holy site and Josephus wrote that the design of the Samaritan Temple was based on the Temple of Jerusalem.

However in about 129 BC, a rebel Jewish army led by John Hyrcanus I invaded Israel and destroyed their place of worship and this action resulted in a bitter hatred between Samaritans and Jews that continued until the time of Jesus.

So it was into this Jewish society living under Roman oppression that Jesus would preach for three years. It was a fractured society where Sadducees and Pharisees were forever arguing and where Jews and Samaritans hated each other.

In this hostile environment Jews and Gentiles didn't freely associate either and the Jews were suffering as a result of punitive taxation by both the Romans and King Herod.

The Jewish population was also living under the burden of having to comply with 613 Mitzvot or 'commandments' from the Torah and they had lost all true spirituality as a result.

However they were living in hope of the arrival of the Messiah as the prophets had foretold, a Messiah who would free them from all this oppression.

The gospels tell us that Magi, practitioners of Zoroastrianism from the East, had informed Herod the Great that a King of Israel was about to be born. In his attempts to prevent a threat to his power base, he ordered the massacre of every male baby aged two years and younger in Jerusalem and its vicinity.

It's unclear how many babies died in this infanticide but Joseph fled with Mary and Jesus into Egypt and stayed there until Herod's death, when they returned to Nazareth.

Little else is written about Jesus' early life although Luke mentions his circumcision and that he was separated from his family after the Passover Feast at the age of twelve and was found four days later in the Temple, sitting with the teachers of the Law.

The next information we have is his baptism by John the Baptist and that he spent forty days in the desert after his baptism before returning to Nazareth. Jesus worked as a carpenter until he began preaching and Luke records that Jesus was about thirty years of age when he began his ministry.

The first public miracle recorded was the conversion of between 450 and 690 litres of water into wine at a wedding feast at Cana in Galilee.

There was reluctance to pay Roman taxes as well as the taxes to King Herod and Mark wrote that Jesus was questioned about this issue by the Pharisees. Later, at his trial before Pilate, the chief priests presented false evidence that he'd encouraged people not to pay their taxes, which was patently untrue.

Mark 12:13: Later they sent some of the Pharisees and Herodians to Jesus to catch him in his words. They came to him and said, "Teacher, we know you are a man of integrity. You aren't swayed by men, because you pay no attention to who they are; but you teach the way of God in accordance with the truth. Is it right to pay taxes to Caesar or not? Should we pay or shouldn't we?"

But Jesus knew their hypocrisy. "Why are you trying to trap me? He asked. Bring me a denarius and let me look at it." They brought the coin, and he asked them, "Whose portrait is this? And who's inscription?"

"Caesar's," they replied.

Then Jesus said to them, "Give to Caesar what is Caesar's and to God what is God's." And they were amazed at him.

According to the Gospels Jesus was crucified for claiming to be the Messiah, which constituted blasphemy to the Jews and carried the death penalty under Jewish law. Matthew, Mark and Luke all recorded this in their gospels.

Matthew 26:63: The high priest said to him, "I charge you under oath by the living God: Tell us if you are the Christ, the Son of God."

"Yes, it is as you say," Jesus replied. "But I say to all of you: In future you will see the Son of Man sitting at the right of the Mighty One and coming on the clouds of heaven."

Then the high priest tore his clothes and said, "He has spoken blasphemy! Why do we need any more witnesses? Look, now you have heard the blasphemy. What do you think?"

"He is worthy of death," they answered. Then they spat in his face and struck him with their fists.

To pagan Romans, a claim by someone to have been the Christ would have been meaningless as they had their own Gods and belief system. However, as the charges relating to Christ brought before Pilate carried no weight with him (hence he said "take him and try him by your own laws") the chief priests and elders shifted the emphasis to insurrection.

It's clear from the writings of historians and the gospel writers that Pilate did not believe Jesus was guilty of anything serious at all, hence the public washing of hands.

However the threat of rioting couldn't be ignored and Pilate realised that this would result in significant bloodshed, so he ultimately passed the death sentence.

There were several means of carrying out the death penalty, but one of the most painful deaths would have been by crucifixion and this method of execution had officially been adopted by the Romans in the 1st century BC, especially for slaves.

It was also used for mass executions after revolts as a means of discouraging further uprisings. For example, six thousand slaves who took part in the rebellion of Spartacus from 73 to 71 BC were crucified along the Appian Way, from Rome to Capua.

Josephus described Varus, the Roman Legate of Syria as having used crucifixion to take revenge on those who had taken part in another uprising in 4 BC.

'Upon this, Varus sent a part of his army into the country, to seek out those that had been the authors of the revolt; and when they were discovered, he punished some of them that were most guilty, and some he dismissed: now the number of those that were crucified on this account were two thousand.' (**Antiquities 17: Book 10**)

After the death of Jesus, these tensions between Jews and Romans persisted and three years later Pilate ordered a brutal attack on Samaritan pilgrims who were visiting their sacred site of Mount Gerizim.

As with conflicts to this day, Pilate's rationale for ordering the attack appears to have been caused by flawed intelligence that he'd been given. It seems that a foreigner who visited Mount Gerizim began spreading rumours, probably in conjunction with a number of accomplices, that he had the power to locate the sacred vessels that had been hidden somewhere on the mountain by Moses many centuries before.

The Samaritans were enraged by what they saw as attempts to desecrate their most holy site and rose up in large numbers, many of them carrying weapons, looking for the seer.

Pilate received word of an 'uprising' and thought that the Samaritans were using the story of the false prophet as a cover for some more sinister plot and duly sent his army in to regain control, which resulted in a massacre.

The Samaritans complained of this atrocity to Vitellius, the Legate of Syria, stating that it hadn't been an uprising at all and Vitellius reported their complaint through to Rome.

For ordering the attack on the Samaritans, Pilate was called to give an account of himself to the Emperor Tiberius in Rome in 36 AD, but before he reached the city Tiberius had died.

The new Emperor Caligula went on to punish Pilate but the records aren't definitive as to whether he was punished for the attack on the Samaritans, or for some other failings relating to his administration of the province.

It's generally thought that he was banished with his wife Claudia Procula to Vienne in Gaul, but there's another tradition that he drank poison during Caligula's reign, possibly a few years later in 39 AD.

Eusebius in his work 'Church History' wrote that Pilate had in fact taken poison but this isn't definitive as he was quoting the writings of earlier and unfortunately unnamed writers.

Taxation was one of the main causes of the devastating Jewish Roman war which lasted from 66-70 AD and which culminated in a 6 month siege of Jerusalem.

Jesus had in fact prophesied the complete destruction of the city as he carried his cross along the Via Dolorosa to Calvary.

As he approached Jerusalem and saw the city, he wept over it and said, "If you, even you, had only known on this day what would bring you peace - but now it is hidden from your eyes. The days will come upon you when your enemies will build an embankment against you and encircle you and hem you in on every side. They will dash you to the ground, you and the children within your walls. They will not leave one stone on another, because you did not recognise the time of God's coming to you." **(Luke 19:41)**

In the middle of the war, on the 9th of June 68 AD, Emperor Nero committed suicide and Vespasian was forced to give up command of the Roman army as a leadership challenge had developed in Rome.

Vespasian would be appointed emperor the very next year, but in the meantime responsibility for taking the city of Jerusalem fell to his son Titus.

Three legions surrounded Jerusalem to the west and a fourth legion was positioned on the Mount of Olives on the east of the city. It's estimated that Titus had 70,000 men surrounding the city and that the Jews had between 30,000 and 40,000 fighting men at their disposal.

Two of the outer city walls were eventually breached but the Zealots held out for a time in the Antonia fortress and in the Temple of Jerusalem itself.

Titus had ordered that the Temple be saved as he planned on converting it into a Roman Temple in honour of the emperor, but it was soon engulfed in the fires spreading throughout the city.

The siege ended with the complete destruction of Jerusalem and its Temple in 70 AD and there was a terrible slaughter of the rebels and the starving residents of Jerusalem who were trapped within the city walls.

In an incredible coincidence, the second temple was set ablaze on 10th August, the very day that the first temple built by Solomon had been burned to the ground by the King of Babylon in 586 BC.

Tacitus put the number of dead at 600,000 and Josephus described the carnage in his work '**The Jewish War**':

"The slaughter within was even more dreadful than the spectacle from without. Men and women, old and young, insurgents and priests, those who fought and those who entreated mercy, were hewn down in indiscriminate carnage. The number of the slain exceeded that of the slayers. The legionaries had to clamber over heaps of dead to carry on the work of extermination."

He also wrote that after the siege of 70 AD, Titus ordered mass crucifixions 'out of rage' and that the soldiers showed extreme cruelty and crucified the Jews on the crosses in a variety of different positions.

The temple and most of the city walls were levelled to their foundations just as Jesus had prophesied.

Some Zealots held out at Masada, a fortress built on top of a rock plateau with cliffs 400 metres high on the eastern approach and 91 metres high to the west.

They lived here until 73 AD, but just as the Roman army was about to enter the stronghold on a siege ramp they'd constructed, the defenders committed suicide to avoid falling into Roman hands.

The massacre at Jerusalem and the destruction of the temple effectively resulted in the end of the Israelite nation until modern times.

- Chapter 7 -
1st piece of evidence: The Messianic Prophecies

The following are the biblical prophecies about the Messiah which were written between one thousand and five hundred and twenty years before the birth of Jesus.

King David

The first two prophecies were made by King David who was born around 1040 BC and who ruled the Israelites for forty years until his death in 970 BC, by which time he'd successfully united all the tribes of Israel.

David had intended to build a great temple to honour God and to house the Ark of the Covenant which he'd brought to Jerusalem, but ultimately this colossal building project fell to his son Solomon. David is accredited with having written many of the Psalms.

Psalm 22:16: They have pierced my hands and my feet. I can count all my bones; people stare and gloat over me. They divide my garments among them and cast lots for my clothing.

This prophecy is utterly remarkable, not just because it was written about 1000 years before Jesus was born, but because it referred to the Messiah dying by crucifixion.

The earliest recorded use of crucifixion in history was in 519 BC, when Darius I of Persia crucified 3000 political opponents in Babylon, so this was 450 to 500 years after David made the prophecy!

Just as stated in the prophecy, the authors of the gospels wrote that Jesus was crucified and that the four soldiers at the crucifixion cast lots for his clothing.

Psalm 16:10: ... because you will not abandon me to the grave, nor will you let your Holy One see decay.

According to the gospels the grave of Jesus was found to be empty on the Sunday morning after his crucifixion the previous Friday and so he wasn't abandoned to the grave and his body did not see decay.

Isaiah

The next three prophecies were made by the great prophet Isaiah who lived from around 740 to 680 BC and who prophesied for at least four of the Kings of Judah. Rabbinic tradition holds that he was martyred by being sawn in two on the instruction of King Manasseh, but there's no real biblical or historical evidence to support this event. The first prophecy of Isaiah was made 700 years before the recorded birth date of Jesus and the name Immanuel translates as 'God with us.'

Isaiah 7:14: Therefore the Lord himself will give you a sign: The virgin will be with child and will give birth to a son, and will call him Immanuel.

The New Testament writings about Jesus indicate that his mother was a virgin, as is clear from Matthew 1:18:

'This is how the birth of Jesus Christ came about: his mother Mary was pledged to be married to Joseph, but before they came together, she was found to be with a child through the Holy Spirit.'

The next prophecy of Isaiah related to the miracles that would be worked by the Messiah who was to come into the World.

Isaiah 35:5: Then will the eyes of the blind be opened and the ears of the deaf unstopped. Then will the lame leap like a deer and the mute tongue shout for joy.

According to several non-Christian historians from antiquity and the New Testament writings, Jesus produced a staggering array of miracles including the healing of deaf, dumb and blind people, as well as the healing of paralytics.

Isaiah's next prophecy concerned how the Messiah would die and that he would die as a ransom for our sins.

Isaiah 53:5: But he was pierced for our transgressions, he was crushed for our iniquities.

Jesus, according to both Christian and non-Christian historical writers, was crucified and he's recorded as having said at the last supper that he would suffer death in order to establish a covenant for the forgiveness of sins.

Matthew 6:27: Then he took the cup, gave thanks and offered it to them, saying, "Drink from it all of you. This is my blood of the covenant, which is poured out for many for the forgiveness of sins."

Micah

The next Old Testament prophet of interest is Micah, who predicted the birth town of the Messiah. Micah was a contemporary of Isaiah and he lived from about 750 to 696 BC and prophesied from around 737 BC until his death.

Predicting the birthplace of the Messiah is his most startling prophecy but he also predicted the destruction of Jerusalem by the Babylonians, which happened in 586 BC.

Micah 5:2: But you, Bethlehem Ephrathah, though you are small among the clans of Judah, out of you will come for me one who will be ruler over Israel, whose origins are from old, from ancient times (or from days of eternity).

The word Ephrath means fertile. So Micah predicted that the Messiah would be born in Bethlehem, a tiny and insignificant town with a population of only several hundred people. And this prophecy was also proved right because this is precisely where Jesus was born according to the Gospels of Matthew and Luke.

Zechariah

Then there is Zechariah, who wrote the following between 520 and 518 BC regarding the betrayal of the Messiah.

Zechariah 11:12: I told them, "If you think it best, give me my pay; but if not, keep it." So they paid me thirty pieces of silver. And the Lord said to me, "Throw it to the potter"- the handsome price at which they priced me! So I took the thirty pieces of silver and threw them into the house of the Lord to the potter.

According to the gospels, Jesus was indeed betrayed by Judas for thirty pieces of silver. He was later filled with remorse and threw them into the temple and the chief priests used the money to buy the potter's field where foreigners could be buried.

Matthew 27:3: When Judas, who had betrayed him, saw that Jesus was condemned, he was seized with remorse and returned the thirty silver coins to the chief priests and the elders.

"I have sinned," he said, "for I have betrayed innocent blood."

"What is that to us?" they replied. "That's your responsibility."

So Judas threw the money into the temple and left. Then he went away and hanged himself.

The chief priests picked up the coins and said, "It is against the law to put this money into the treasury, since it is blood money." So they decided to use the money to buy the potter's field as a burial place for foreigners.

Given the fact that these prophecies were written between 520 and 1000 years before Jesus lived, they are quite remarkable. What's the probability of these highly specific prophecies made by four different prophets and spanning one thousand years of history, all being manifest in the person of Jesus?

The Messianic prophecies are therefore the first piece of evidence that support the divinity of Jesus.

- Chapter 8 -
2nd piece of evidence: The miracles worked by Jesus

It's logical to expect that the presence of the Son of God on Earth would be accompanied by inexplicable and wondrous acts and these were prophesied by Isaiah. The vast array of miracles Jesus worked were of course described in the gospels, but they were also mentioned by historians from antiquity such as Josephus and Tertullian.

"Jesus went throughout Galilee, teaching in their synagogues, preaching the good news of the kingdom, and healing every disease and sickness among the people. News about him spread all over Syria, and people brought to him all who were ill with various diseases, those suffering severe pain, the demon-possessed, those having seizures, and the paralysed, and he healed them." (Matthew 4:23)

Josephus made a reference to these miracles in a passage called the **Testimonium flavianum**, which is in book 18 of his work 'Antiquities of the Jews,' which was written around 93 AD.

'Now there was about this time Jesus, a wise man, if it be lawful to call him a man, for he was a doer of wonderful works, a teacher of such men as receive the truth with pleasure. He drew over to him both many of the Jews, and many of the Gentiles.'

Tertullian gave a much more detailed description of these miracles in chapter 21 of '**The Apologeticum**' which he wrote in 197 AD.

'As, then, under the force of their pre-judgment, they had convinced themselves from His lowly guise that Christ was no more than man, it followed from that, as a necessary consequence, that they should hold Him a magician from the powers which He displayed, expelling devils from men by a word, restoring vision to the blind, cleansing the leprous, reinvigorating the paralytic, summoning the dead to life again, making the very elements of nature obey Him, stilling the storms and walking on the sea; proving that He was the Logos of God, that primordial first-begotten Word, accompanied by power and reason, and based on Spirit, that He who was now doing all things by His word, and He who had done that of old, were one and the same.'

Jesus was unique because he was the only prophet from the time of Moses through to John the Baptist that had ever claimed to be the Son of God and he also stated that he would raise himself from the dead as proof of his divinity.

Other prophets such as Moses, Elijah and Elisha are accredited with having performed miracles long before the time of Jesus. Elijah for example raised the son of a widow to life, as is recorded in 1 Kings 17:22 and he called fire down from the sky to kill a captain and fifty soldiers on two separate occasions (2 Kings 1:10).

The prophet Elisha worked the miracle of multiplication, where he allowed a poor widow to multiply a tiny volume of oil into a vast quantity in order to pay off all her debts (2 Kings 4:1).

Elisha also multiplied bread in order to feed a hundred men in 2 Kings 4:43 and he's also recorded as having raised a young boy to life in 2 Kings 4:32.

Saint Paul is also credited with having raised a young man named Eutychus to life, after he'd fallen asleep and dropped from an upper window while he was preaching in Troas (Acts 20:7).

Again, the apostle Peter raised a lady named Tabitha from death while he was in the city of Joppa, as is recorded in Acts 9:40.

However the miracles attributed to Jesus are unique in history in both their diversity and their scale and these signs were performed by him as supporting evidence that he was the Messiah.

Many of the Pharisees witnessed these miracles first hand, but were so proud and intransigent that they still refused to accept that this uneducated carpenter, who'd grown up in front of them, could possibly be the Son of God.

There's a tendency to think that these accounts were possibly exaggerated, but we shouldn't for a moment believe this to be the case, as the miracles were recorded by both Christian and non-Christian authors and historians.

Some of the miracles involved the healing of incurables, but others prove that Jesus had power over life itself, as well as power over the very forces of nature.

Changing water into wine

>On the third day a wedding took place at Cana in Galilee. Jesus' mother was there, and Jesus and his disciples had also been invited to the wedding. When the wine was gone, Jesus' mother said to him, "They have no more wine."

"Dear woman, why do you involve me?" Jesus replied.

"My time has not yet come."

Nearby stood six stone water jars, the kind used by the Jews for ceremonial washing, each holding from seventy-five to a hundred and fifteen litres.

Jesus said to the servants, "Fill the jars with water"; so they filled them to the brim. Then he told them, "Now draw some out and take it to the master of the banquet."

They did so, and the master of the banquet tasted the water that had been turned into wine. He did not realise where it had come from, though the servants who had drawn the water knew. Then he called the bridegroom aside and said, "Everyone brings out the choice wine first and then the cheaper wine after the guests have had too much to drink; but you have saved the best till now." **(John 2:1)**

In this account Jesus converted between 450 and 690 litres of water into a high quality wine and we could argue that transubstantiation had taken place as he'd clearly brought about a change of substance. As the volume hadn't increased, Jesus had actually changed the molecular structure of the water into wine.

Many find it difficult to understand the Catholic teaching of transubstantiation of the bread wafers at the words of consecration, but this miracle is an example of a substance being changed instantly at his command.

It's interesting that the Eastern Orthodox Church holds that the apostle Simon the Zealot was the bridegroom at this wedding!

Healing of a leper

>A man with leprosy came to him and begged him on his knees, "If you are willing, you can make me clean."

Filled with compassion, Jesus reached out his hand and touched the man. "I am willing," he said. "Be clean!" Immediately the leprosy left him and he was cured." **(Mark 1:40)**

Leprosy was not just a painful and life threatening disease, but it also resulted in the sufferer being ostracised from the community. Mosaic Law had strict regulations on how people with contagious skin diseases had to be treated and these are found in the books of Leviticus and Numbers.

Leviticus 13:45: The person with such an infectious disease must wear torn clothes, let his hair be unkempt, cover the lower part of his face and cry out 'Unclean! Unclean!' As long as he has the infection he remains unclean. He must live alone; he must live outside the camp.

Numbers 5:1: The Lord said to Moses, "Command the Israelites to send away from the camp anyone who has an infectious skin disease or who is ceremonially unclean because of a dead body."

Jesus was full of compassion on seeing the wretched sight before him, begging on his knees and he healed him. What would have been remarkable to the crowds wouldn't just be the healing itself, but the fact that Jesus touched the man and that he was unconcerned about being defiled for having touched a leper.

Healing of a paralytic

>When Jesus had entered Capernaum, a centurion came to him, asking for help. "Lord," he said, "my servant lies at home paralysed and in terrible suffering."

Jesus said to him, "I will go and heal him."

The centurion replied, "Lord, I do not deserve to have you come under my roof. But just say the word, and my servant will be healed. For I myself am a man under authority, with soldiers under me. I tell this one, 'Go,' and he goes; and that one, 'Come,' and he comes. I say to my servant, 'Do this,' and he does it."

When Jesus heard this, he was astonished and said to those following him, "I tell you the truth, I have not found anyone in Israel with such great faith. I say to you that many will come from the east and the west, and will take their places at the feast with Abraham, Isaac and Jacob in the kingdom of heaven. But the subjects of the kingdom will be thrown outside, into the darkness, where there will be weeping and gnashing of teeth."

Then Jesus said to the centurion, "Go! It will be done just as you believed it would." And his servant was healed at that very hour. **(Matthew 8:5)**

This was a rare encounter between Jesus and a centurion and the soldier surprised Jesus by the depth of his faith, as he understood that Jesus didn't physically have to travel to the place where his servant was, but could just will him to be healed. As Jesus wasn't present with the servant but was still able to heal him, it shows that physical contact was unnecessary for him to effect a miraculous healing.

Jesus warns the Pharisees that the chosen people wouldn't accept his message for salvation but that others would. The Edict of Milan of 313 AD marked the end of persecution against Christians and 11 years later Constantine became the sole ruler of the Roman Empire and adopted Christianity as his own religion. From then on the whole empire began moving away from paganism as it embraced Christianity.

Raising a young dead man to life in Nain

>Soon afterwards, Jesus went to a town called Nain, and his disciples and a large crowd went along with him. As he approached the town gate, a dead person was being carried out – the only son of his mother, and she was a widow. And a large crowd from the town was with her.

When the Lord saw her, his heart went out to her and he said, "Don't cry."

Then he went up and touched the coffin, and those carrying it stood still. He said, "Young man, I say to you, get up!"

The dead man sat up and began to talk, and Jesus gave him back to his mother.

They were all filled with awe and praised God. "A great prophet has appeared among us," they said. **(Luke 7:11)**

This was the first of three people that Jesus raised from the dead and the miracle demonstrates that he had power over life itself.

Healing Bernice of persistent bleeding

>Just then a woman who had been subject to bleeding for twelve years came up behind him and touched the edge of his cloak. She said to herself, "If I only touch his cloak, I will be healed."

Jesus turned and saw her. "Take heart, daughter," he said, "your faith has healed you." And the woman was healed from that moment. **(Matthew 9:20)**

In this miracle it was only necessary for the woman to touch the edge of his cloak to be healed and in Mark's account it states that Jesus was aware that 'power had gone out from him,' so during the healing process there was a transfer of power that Jesus could feel.

We know that this woman's name was Bernice, not from the New Testament gospel writers, but from the apocryphal Gospel of Nicodemus. Bernice was a woman of immense courage and she was breaking protocol by approaching and touching Jesus because her bleeding would have rendered her ceremonially unclean.

Women were also not permitted to give evidence at trial, but this didn't stop Bernice at the trial of Jesus and according to the Gospel of Nicodemus she cried out to Pilate in his defence, but was silenced by the chief priests and elders.

The healing of two blind men

>As Jesus went on from there, two blind men followed him, calling out, "Have mercy on us, Son of David!"

When he had gone indoors, the blind men came to him, and he asked them, "Do you believe that I am able to do this?"

"Yes, Lord" they replied.

Then he touched their eyes and said, "According to your faith will it be done to you," and their sight was restored. **(Matthew 9:27)**

It's interesting that they called Jesus 'Son of David,' as the Messiah was to be a descendent of King David and it shows that they had great respect for him or possibly even believed that he was the Messiah.

The Gospel of Nicodemus records one blind man who had been healed by Jesus trying to defend him before Pilate and it may well have been one of these two men. This is because at the trial the blind man stated that he had called out to Jesus, "Have mercy on me, O son of David."

Raising the twelve year old daughter of Jairus to life

>While Jesus was still speaking, some men came from the house of Jairus, the synagogue ruler. "Your daughter is dead," they said. "Why bother the teacher any more?"

Ignoring what they said, Jesus told the synagogue ruler, "Don't be afraid; just believe." He did not let anyone follow him except Peter, James and John the brother of James. When they came to the home of the synagogue ruler, Jesus saw a commotion, with people crying and wailing loudly.

He went in and said to them, "Why all this commotion and wailing? The child is not dead but asleep."

But they laughed at him. After he put them all out, he took the child's father and mother and the disciples who were with him, and went in where the child was. He took her by the hand and said to her, "Talitha koum!" (Which means, "Little girl, I say to you, get up!")

Immediately the girl stood up and walked around (she was twelve years old). At this they were completely astonished. **(Mark 5:35)**

Jesus took his trusted trio of Peter, James and John with him into the room of the twelve year old girl and raised her from the dead in front of Jairus and his wife. News of this would have spread quickly to the chief priests and elders of the Sanhedrin in Jerusalem, as Jairus was himself a synagogue ruler.

Feeding 5000 men through the miracle of multiplication

>As evening approached, the disciples came to him and said, "This is a remote place, and it's already getting late. Send the crowds away, so they can go to the villages and buy themselves some food."

Jesus replied, "They do not need to go away. You give them something to eat."

"We have here only five loaves of bread and two fish," they answered.

"Bring them here to me," he said. And he directed the people to sit down on the grass. Taking the five loaves and the two fish and looking up to heaven, he gave thanks and broke the loaves. Then he gave them to the disciples, and the disciples gave them to the people. They all ate and were satisfied, and the disciples picked up twelve basketfuls of broken pieces that were left over. The number of those who ate was about five thousand men, besides women and children. **(Matthew 14:15)**

The miracle here was different to that at Cana because in this case Jesus replicated the same material about a thousand times over. John wrote that Jesus asked Philip as a test, 'Where shall we buy bread for these people to eat?' to which he replied, 'Eight months wages would not buy enough bread for each one to have a bite!'

If women and children are included in the number present, then Jesus must surely have fed at least fifteen thousand people.

The healing of countless people who touched his clothing

After this great miracle Jesus went up a mountainside to pray alone and in the early hours of the next morning he came down from the mountain and walked out onto the Sea of Galilee towards the apostles in their boat. They sailed to the northwest shore of the lake and landed at the town of Gennesaret, where another large crowd had gathered to meet him.

Matthew's gospel records that 'People brought all their sick to him and begged him to let the sick just touch the edge of his cloak, and all who touched him were healed.' **(Matthew 14:35)**

Incredibly, in the middle of all these wondrous signs in front of tens of thousands of people, the response of the Pharisees and teachers of the law was to question Jesus as to why his disciples hadn't ritually washed their hands before eating!

The feeding of 4000 men through the miracle of multiplication

>Great crowds came to him, bringing the lame, the blind, the crippled, the dumb and many others, and laid them at his feet; and he healed them. The people were amazed when they saw the dumb speaking, the crippled made well, the lame walking and the blind seeing.

Jesus called his disciples to him and said, "I have compassion for these people; they have already been with me three days and have nothing to eat. I do not want to send them away hungry, or they may collapse on the way."

His disciples answered, "Where could we get enough bread in this remote place to feed such a crowd?"

"How many loaves do you have?" Jesus asked.

"Seven," they replied, "and a few small fish."

He told the crowd to sit down on the ground. Then he took the seven loaves and the fish, and when he had given thanks, he broke them and gave them to the disciples, and they in turn to the people.

They all ate and were satisfied. Afterwards the disciples picked up seven basketfuls of broken pieces that were left over. The number of those who ate was four thousand, besides women and children. **(Matthew 15:30)**

The massive crowds were clearly so in awe of what they were witnessing that they forgot to buy themselves food and it's surprising that at this stage, the apostles still periodically doubted Jesus.

But again he worked a miracle of multiplication and presumably fed at least twelve thousand people including women and children.

The healing of ten lepers

>Now on his way to Jerusalem, Jesus traveled along the border between Samaria and Galilee. As he was going into a village, ten men who had leprosy met him. They stood at a distance and called out in a loud voice, "Jesus, Master, have pity on us!"

When he saw them, he said, "Go, show yourselves to the priests."

And as they went, they were cleansed. One of them, when he saw he was healed, came back, praising God in a loud voice. He threw himself at Jesus' feet and thanked him - and he was a Samaritan.

Jesus asked, "Were not all ten cleansed? Where are the other nine? Has no one returned to give praise to God except this foreigner?" Then he said to him, "Rise and go; your faith has made you well." **(Luke 17:11)**

The ten lepers were living outside the village as they were required to do by law and Leviticus 14 outlined the complicated process for ceremonial cleansing, which involved several examinations by the priests.

It's remarkable that the leper who returned to give thanks was a Samaritan, as this community avoided any contact with the Jews. At the trial of Jesus one leper is recorded as having spoken out in his defence and although we don't know for sure which leper it was, it may well have been this man. During his ministry Jesus tried to get the Jews to give up their prejudice towards the Samaritans and this is evidenced in the parable of the Good Samaritan and also in his encounter with the Samaritan woman at Jacob's well.

The healing of a boy at Capernaum

>Once more he visited Cana in Galilee, where he had turned the water into wine. And there was a certain royal official whose son lay sick at Capernaum. When this man heard that Jesus had arrived in Galilee from Judea, he went to him and begged him to come and heal his son, who was close to death.

"Unless you people see miraculous signs and wonders," Jesus told him, "you will never believe."

The royal official said, "Sir, come down before my child dies."

Jesus replied, "You may go. Your son will live."

The man took Jesus at his word and departed. While he was still on the way, his servants met him with the news that his boy was living. When he inquired as to the time when his son got better, they said to him, "The fever left him yesterday at the seventh hour."

Then the father realised that this was the exact time at which Jesus had said to him, "Your son will live." So he and all his household believed. **(John 4:46)**

Of the gospel writers, it's only John who used Roman chronology, which is the same system as we use today. So the seventh hour is seven hours after midnight or 7 am.

Matthew, Mark and Luke used Jewish chronology, where the day was split into three hour periods called 'hours' and 'watches.' So the third hour was 6 to 9am; the sixth hour was 9 to 12 mid-day, the ninth hour was mid-day to 3pm and the twelfth hour was 3 to 6 pm.

The first watch was from 6 to 9 pm; the second watch was 9 pm to midnight, the third watch was midnight to 3am and the fourth watch was from 3 to 6 am.

This is an important detail as it explains the different times given by John in his gospel account of the trial and crucifixion of Jesus when compared to the other gospel writers!

This miracle is remarkable in that the boy was healed in Capernaum which was 42 kilometres away from where Jesus was in Cana.

Healing of a paralytic at the pool named Bethesda in Jerusalem

>Some time later, Jesus went up to Jerusalem for a feast of the Jews. Now there is in Jerusalem near the Sheep Gate a pool, which in Aramaic is called Bethesda and which is surrounded by five covered colonnades. Here a great number of disabled people used to lie – the blind, the lame, the paralysed.

One who was there had been an invalid for thirty-eight years. When Jesus saw him lying there and learned that he had been in this condition for a long time, he asked him, "Do you want to get well?"

"Sir," the invalid replied, "I have no one to help me into the pool when the water is stirred. While I am trying to get in, someone else goes down ahead of me."

Then Jesus said to him, "Get up! Pick up your mat and walk."

At once the man was cured; he picked up his mat and walked. The day on which this took place was a Sabbath, and so the Jews said to the man who had been healed, "It is the Sabbath; the law forbids you to carry your mat."

But he replied, "The man who made me well said to me, 'Pick up your mat and walk.'"

So they asked him, "Who is this fellow who told you to pick it up and walk?" The man who was healed had no idea who it was, for Jesus had slipped away into the crowd that was there.

Later Jesus found him at the temple and said to him, "See, you are well again. Stop sinning or something worse may happen to you."

The man went away and told the Jews that it was Jesus who had made him well. **(John 5:1)**

Archaeologists including Schick in the 19th century discovered what appeared to be the remains of this 13 metre deep pool, about 30 metres from St Anne's church in the Muslim quarter of Jerusalem.

The name is thought to be a derivative of the Hebrew or Aramaic beth hesda which means 'house of grace' but in both languages could also mean 'disgrace.' This makes sense as in those days it could have been seen as a place of disgrace with all the invalids by the pool, or alternatively a place of grace because of those who were healed there.

This invalid doesn't appear to have had a congenital condition that caused his paralysis as John wrote that he'd been an invalid for 38 years, as opposed to writing that he'd been crippled from birth. The paralysis may have been caused by a disease or an injury to his spine but Jesus is reported to have healed him in an instant.

Again he was one of the few brave people who shouted out to defend Jesus at his trial before Pilate according to the Gospel of Nicodemus.

The Transfiguration

>After six days Jesus took Peter, James and John with him and led them up a high mountain, where they were all alone. There he was transfigured before them. His clothes became dazzling white, whiter than anyone in the World could bleach them. And there appeared before them Elijah and Moses, who were talking with Jesus.

Peter said to Jesus, "Rabbi, it is good for us to be here. Let us put up three shelters – one for you, one for Moses and one for Elijah." (He did not know what to say, they were so frightened.)

Then a cloud appeared and enveloped them, and a voice came from the cloud: "This is my Son, whom I love. Listen to him!" Suddenly, when they looked round, they no longer saw anyone with them except Jesus. **(Mark 9:2)**

In Matthew's gospel it states that the face of Jesus shone like the sun and Luke also wrote that the appearance of his face changed. Peter, James and John were looking at the transfigured body of Jesus, but they were also looking at two prophets from ancient times physically alive and talking, which was definitive proof to them of life after death.

The raising of Lazarus from the dead

>On his arrival, Jesus found that Lazarus had already been in the tomb for four days. Bethany was less than three kilometres from Jerusalem, and many Jews had come to Martha and Mary to comfort them in the loss of their brother.

When Martha heard that Jesus was coming, she went out to meet him, but Mary stayed at home. "Lord," Martha said to Jesus, "If you had been here, my brother would not have died. But I know that even now God will give you whatever you ask."

Jesus said to her, "Your brother will rise again."

Martha answered, "I know he will rise again in the resurrection at the last day."

Jesus said to her., "I am the resurrection and the life. He who believes in me will live, even though he dies; and whoever lives and believes in me will never die. Do you believe this?"

"Yes, Lord," she told him, "I believe that you are the Christ, the Son of God, who was to come into this world."

And after she had said this, she went back and called her sister Mary aside. "The Teacher is here," she said, "and is asking for you." When Mary heard this, she got up quickly and went to him.

Now Jesus had not yet entered the village, but was still at the place where Martha had met him. When the Jews who had been with Mary in the house, comforting her, noticed how quickly she got up and went out, they followed her, supposing she was going to the tomb to mourn there.

When Mary reached the place where Jesus was and saw him, she fell at his feet and said, "Lord, if you had been here, my brother would not have died."

When Jesus saw her weeping, and the Jews who had come along with her also weeping, he was deeply moved in spirit and troubled. "Where have you laid him?" he asked.

"Come and see, Lord," they replied. Jesus wept. Then the Jews said, "See how he loved him!"

But some of them said, "Could not he who opened the eyes of the blind man have kept this man from dying?"

Jesus, once more deeply moved, came to the tomb. It was a cave with a stone laid across the entrance. "Take away the stone," he said.

"But, Lord," said Martha, the sister of the dead man, "by this time there is a bad odour, for he has been there four days."

Then Jesus said, "Did I not tell you that if you believed, you would see the glory of God?"

So they took away the stone. Then Jesus looked up and said, "Father, I thank you that you have heard me. I knew that you always hear me, but I said this for the benefit of the people standing here, that they may believe that you sent me."

When he had said this, Jesus called out in a loud voice, "Lazarus, come out!"

The dead man came out, his hands and feet wrapped with strips of linen, and a cloth around his face. Jesus said to them, "Take off the grave clothes and let him go."

Therefore many of the Jews who had come to visit Mary and had seen what Jesus did, put their faith in him. But some of them went to the Pharisees and told them what Jesus had done.

Then the chief priests and the Pharisees called a meeting of the Sanhedrin. "What are we accomplishing?" they asked. "Here is this man performing many miraculous signs. If we let him go on like this, everyone will believe in him, and then the Romans will come and take away both our place and our nation."

Then one of them, named Caiaphas, who was high priest that year, spoke up, "You know nothing at all! You do not realise that it is better for you that one man die for the people than the whole nation perish." **(John 11:17)**

This was arguably the greatest miracle performed by Jesus as it definitively showed that he had power over life and it gave tangible evidence that Jesus would raise the elect at the last day as he had taught. The enormous implications of this miracle forced the chief priests to act and so from that day on they plotted to take his life. Jesus performed this miracle very close to the time of his own death and there are clear parallels here between the raising of Lazarus and the resurrection of Jesus himself.

When his tomb was discovered empty on the Sunday morning, the raising of Lazarus would have helped many to see how it was possible for Jesus to have raised himself from death.

Jesus also said that his miracles should be seen as evidence that he was indeed the Son of God.

"Why then do you accuse me of blasphemy because I said, 'I am God's son'? Do not believe me unless I do what my Father does. But if I do it, even though you do not believe me, believe the evidence of the miracles that you may know and understand that the Father is in me, and I in the Father." **(John 10:36)**

These miracles represent the second piece of evidence that point to Jesus being divine and again it's important to remember that the miracles were also described by historians from antiquity.

- Chapter 9 -
Forensic analysis of the death of Jesus

The earliest reference to crucifixion in historical writings was in 519 BC and the practice was only finally abolished under Constantine in 337 AD, out of veneration for Jesus, as he had himself become a Christian.

Crucifixion had also been used by Alexander the Great, who massacred eight thousand people after the siege of Tyre in 332 BC, of which two thousand were reported to have been crucified.

Alexander Jannaeus the King of Judea from 103 to 76 BC is said to have crucified eight hundred Pharisees in Jerusalem after the Judean civil war.

Even during World War II the Japanese army sometimes crucified POW's such as during the construction of the Thailand-Burma railway in 1943. This didn't involve driving nails through the hands and feet but instead the soldiers were tied into place with wire or rope.

The Romans sometimes used just an upright post or Crux simplex, but the more common types were the Crux commissa, which was T shaped i.e. with the beam at the top, and the one Christians are most familiar with, the Crux immissa.

However they sometimes used 'X' shaped or even 'Y' shaped crosses and Cicero described crucifixion as 'a most cruel and disgusting punishment.'

There were several methods of putting criminals to death at the time of Jesus but at his trial the chief priests and elders were shouting for him to be crucified. This method would have given the Jewish authorities the maximum public exposure of the execution, in the hope of stamping out his following altogether.

Jesus, assisted by Simon of Cyrene, had to carry his cross or the beam of his cross through the streets of Jerusalem and this journey would have begun at the Praetorium or Pilate's palace and ended at Golgotha in sight of hundreds of onlookers.

Jesus had criticised the chief priests, often calling them hypocrites in public and he'd frequently challenged their interpretation of The Law.

The chief priests were also concerned that his massive popularity would ultimately result in the Romans clamping down on the Jewish people and possibly withdrawing their privileges and the authority of the Sanhedrin, so for these reasons they wanted him killed.

In history there are rare accounts of people surviving crucifixion, but in most of these cases the guards were involved in releasing the prisoners from the cross.

Josephus wrote that one day he had recognised three rebels hanging on crosses who had earlier fought by his side during the Jewish Roman war. He went to Titus to plead for them and they were taken down from their crosses, with Titus instructing that they be given the 'greatest care' and yet despite this, two of the three still died.

An example from more recent history was that of Herbert James Edwards and two other soldiers who were crucified in 1943 by Japanese troops while building the Thailand-Burma railway.

They'd been caught killing cattle for food and were sentenced to death. The three soldiers were crucified by being hung from a tree by their wrists with wire and then beaten with baseball bats and after the beating they were just left hanging there from the tree to die.

Herbert managed to free his one hand but when the soldiers discovered this they re-hung him, but this time the wire was pushed straight through his hands.

Sixty three hours later, the three soldiers were taken down but only Herbert Edwards survived the ordeal. Remarkably Herbert only died in his native Western Australia in June 2000 at the age of eighty six!

Other cases of soldiers being crucified from bamboo crosses in 1943 emerged at a war crimes tribunal convened after the war.

The gospel accounts indicate that Jesus had been severely beaten and later scourged before his crucifixion. The scourging with a flagrum was administered by between one and six trained lectors and the leather straps of the flagrum had sharp pieces of metal, bone, glass and sometimes hooks knotted at the end.

Under Jewish law the number of strikes was limited to forty but usually ended at thirty nine lashings, but under Roman law there was no restriction on the number of lashes.

The Roman scourging was called a 'half death' as it was designed to bring the victim close to death and this would ensure that criminals would spend less time hanging on their crosses.

In some cases the criminals actually died during the scourging and according to historical records the cuts were so deep that the entrails of the prisoners were sometimes exposed.

Senators, Roman citizens, women and also soldiers, except for the crime of desertion, were generally exempt from scourging. Now the time that a person would survive on the cross would generally be determined by the ferocity of the scourging, the extent of blood loss and the health and physical condition of the prisoner before the punishment began.

The punishment of Jesus was more brutal than usual, in that prior to the flogging Jesus had also been beaten at the house of Caiaphas the high priest and later again by the soldiers at the Praetorium.

Mark 14:65: Then some began to spit at him; they blindfolded him, struck him with their fists, and said, "Prophesy!" And the guards took him and beat him.

Mark 15:16: The soldiers led Jesus away into the palace (that is, the Praetorium) and called together the whole company of soldiers. They put a purple robe on him, then twisted together a crown of thorns and set it on him. And they began to call out to him, "Hail, king of the Jews!" Again and again they struck him on the head with a staff and spat on him.

It's clear that Jesus would have been severely injured as a result of these two beatings and the scourging and he must surely have been on the point of collapse when the heavy cross was placed on his shoulder.

It's uncertain whether Jesus was forced to carry the whole cross (patibulum and stipes) or just the beam of the cross and the weight of a full cross was estimated at 135 Kg, whereas the crossbeam or patibulum is estimated to have weighed about 45 Kg.

Three of the gospel accounts record that a man named Simon from Cyrene was summoned to help him carry his cross, which indicates that Jesus was by this stage completely exhausted and falling down.

Mark 15:21: A certain man from Cyrene, Simon, the father of Alexander and Rufus, was passing by on his way in from the country, and they forced him to carry the cross.

It's interesting that John, who was the only apostle present at the crucifixion site of Calvary, doesn't mention Simon of Cyrene at all but does record Jesus carrying his own cross.

John 19:17: Carrying his own cross, he went out to the place of the Skull (which in Aramaic is called Golgotha).

So Jesus initially carried the cross, but due to his exhausted state, the soldiers then forced Simon to carry it and this is unlikely to have been an act of kindness. As the whole company of soldiers had gathered around Jesus to beat him in the Praetorium it's likely that the soldiers guarding him on the road to Calvary were some of these very same men.

So the motivation for them forcing Simon to assist with the carrying of the cross was probably the soldier's fear of being sanctioned had Jesus died prior to crucifixion.

Tensions would have been running high and the officials may have wanted the crucifixion over with quickly in case rioting broke out on the streets.

The chief priests and elders were clearly concerned about this as they'd arrested Jesus in the middle of the night and tried him before the Sanhedrin in the early hours of the morning.

Before being crucified, Jesus was offered wine mixed with the bitter herb Myrrh, which he refused to drink. This herb is made from the resin of the low growing Myrrh tree and had been used for centuries in Egypt as part of the mummification process.

It was highly valued and was one of the three gifts presented to Jesus at his birth and it's still used in Chinese medicine today to improve circulation of the blood, to treat traumatic injuries and to reduce swelling.

But as well as easing pain, Myrrh also breaks up congealed blood and would prevent the wounds congealing, thereby increasing the blood loss and hastening death.

Prior to the cross being erected in place, nails were driven through the palms of the hands (or in later times, the wrists) and the feet of the victim, which would have caused excruciating pain and indeed the word excruciating means 'out of crucifying.'

The large nails are likely to have severed the Deep Palmar Arch, which is the main artery supplying the hand. In the region of the foot where the nails would have passed are several blood vessels and either the Arcuate artery, the Lateral Tarsal artery or the Dorsalis pedis artery would likely have been severed.

Only one skeleton of a person who had died of crucifixion in the first century AD has so far been found, which is unsurprising as the Romans generally forbade burial and the corpses were just left to decay and be eaten by scavengers and maggots.

However Jewish law required that the bodies of Jews be taken down from the cross and buried before sundown and this custom in Mosaic Law can be traced back to Deuteronomy 21:22:

'If a man guilty of a capital offence is put to death and his body is hung on a tree, you must not leave his body on the tree overnight. Be sure to bury him that same day, because anyone who is hung on a tree is under God's curse.'

The skeleton was found at Giv'at ha-Mivtar in northeast Jerusalem in 1968 and the heel of the skeleton still had a bent nail through it, which would have been difficult to remove.

It's thought that the Romans re-used nails from crucifixions because iron was in short supply at that time. Nails from crucifixions were also sought after as amulets, as people at the time believed them to have healing powers.

On this particular skeleton it appeared that the nails had been driven through the sides of the heels into opposite sides of the upright of the cross.

The nail found in this skeleton was 11.5cm long and tapered with a square base which was about 1cm across, which is many times thicker than an average nail of today. Both legs of the victim had been broken, but for some reason the body had been permitted a proper burial.

At the tip of the nail was some Olive wood, indicating that the upright was made from the wood of an Olive tree and as these are low growing trees the victim was probably crucified not far above the height of an average person.

Hanging on a cross with arms outstretched makes breathing progressively more difficult and its thought that this would ultimately result in suffocation.

For this reason the Romans sometimes affixed a wooden foot block or suppendaneum to the cross, to allow the victim to push against it in order to catch a breath. The Greek word for this foot block was a hypopodium.

In doing this it would have been necessary for the victims to push themselves up against the nails through their feet, thereby causing terrible pain and blood loss.

Some crosses had a small seat or 'sedile' affixed to them about half way down the vertical beam and Justin Martyr wrote that the cross of Jesus had "five extremities, two in length, two in breadth, and one in the middle, on which the person rests who is fixed by the nails."

So this description possibly indicates the presence of a sedile on the cross of Jesus.

It's interesting that Irenaeus, who lived from around 125 to 202 AD, also described the cross of Jesus as having had five extremities and not four.

Irenaeus became the Bishop of Lyons, but when he was young he met Polycarp and listened to his preachings. Now Polycarp was a disciple of the apostle John and John later appointed him as Bishop of Smyrna.

John was the only apostle actually present at the crucifixion and would have known exactly what the cross of Jesus looked like and we can be certain that he would have passed on this information to Polycarp. So it's not inconceivable that Irenaeus came to know the structure of the cross that Jesus was crucified on from Polycarp himself.

Polycarp suffered a martyr's death for refusing to burn incense to the Roman Emperor, probably in the year 156 AD, by being burned at the stake and then speared when the flames had no effect on his body.

There's some debate as to what the eventual cause of death is during crucifixion, but the main causes are either suffocation due to difficulty in breathing; the rupturing of the heart as a result of the acute build up of fluid in the heart membrane, heart failure or pulmonary embolism.

Another cause could be hypovolemia, which is decreased blood plasma volume as distinct from overall total blood volume loss.

In the case of the rupturing of the heart, a large amount of fluid that had accumulated in the membrane would suddenly be released into the thoracic cavity.

To hasten death the Romans usually bludgeoned the legs with an iron club or crurifragium and this could result in sudden death through severe traumatic shock.

If the victim survived the immediate trauma he would soon succumb anyway, because with broken tibia bones it would be impossible to push against the nails or the foot block and he would therefore be unable to breath. It's uncertain whether foot blocks were routinely fitted to the crosses or not.

According to the gospel accounts Jesus was on the cross for several hours before he let out a loud shout and died.

Mark 15:25: It was the **third hour** when they crucified him.

Mark 15:33: And at the **ninth hour** Jesus cried out in a loud voice, "Eloi, Eloi, lama sabachthani?"- which means, "My God, my God, why have you forsaken me?"

Mark 15:37: With a loud cry, Jesus breathed his last.

The times given in John's gospel differ from the other gospels as for example John indicates that Pilate's decision to crucify Jesus was made 'about the **sixth hour**.'

So if the decision to crucify Jesus was made about the sixth hour then the actual time when he was crucified would have been a few hours after the sixth hour according to John.

John 19:14: It was the day of Preparation of Passover Week, about the sixth hour. "Here is your King," Pilate said to the Jews.

The most likely explanation for this difference is that John's chronology was according to Roman time where the sixth hour would be 6 am. There's supporting evidence for this elsewhere in John's gospel where he mentions a 'seventh hour' which was not used by Matthew, Mark or Luke in their gospels.

This was in his account of the healing of the son of a royal official that Jesus had met while in Cana. The boy was dying in his home in Capernaum and according to John he was miraculously healed by Jesus despite the fact that the boy was 42 kilometres away.

John 4:52: When he enquired as to the time when his son got better, they said to him, "The fever left him yesterday at the **seventh hour**."

When Jesus uttered the words, 'Eloi, Eloi, lama sabachthani' meaning 'My God, my God, why have you forsaken me?' he may have been making a desperate cry to God but he could also have been reciting the start of Psalm 22.

This psalm contains the words 'they have pierced my hands and my feet. I can count all my bones; people stare and gloat over me. They divide my garments among them and cast lots for my clothing.'

In verse 24 it is written: 'For he has not despised or disdained the suffering of the afflicted one; he has not hidden his face from him but has listened to his cry for help.'

Indeed the whole second part of Psalm 22 is about praise of God.

John's gospel account tells us that as the centurion pierced the side of Jesus with a spear to ensure that he was dead, there came forth a sudden flow of **blood and water** and this is of great significance from a medical perspective.

John 19:33: 'But when they came to Jesus and found that he was already dead, they did not break his legs. Instead, one of the soldiers pierced Jesus' side with a spear, bringing a sudden flow of blood and water. The man who saw it has given testimony, and his testimony is true. He knows that he tells the truth, and he testifies so that you also may believe.'

The sudden flow of blood and water is consistent with the heart membrane having ruptured and the subsequent release of accumulated fluid. Of the gospel writers it's only John who mentions this lancing, but again he was the only apostle actually present at the crucifixion!

The rupturing of the heart membrane would quickly result in death and Mark wrote that Jesus let out a loud cry at the moment of death, which would be consistent with the sudden pain associated with this.

Mark 15:37: 'With a loud cry, Jesus breathed his last.'

It's interesting that John recorded that it was the Jewish chief priests who asked Pilate to have the legs broken so as to ensure death and to prevent the bodies from hanging on the crosses on the Sabbath.

John 19:31: 'Because the Jews did not want the bodies left on the crosses during the Sabbath, they asked Pilate to have the legs broken and the bodies taken down.'

They'd gone to great lengths to have Jesus brought to trial and had only just managed to convince Pilate to have him executed and so it's logical that they wouldn't have taken any chances that could have allowed Jesus to survive the crucifixion.

The scene at Golgotha would have been bustling with activity as Jesus had a massive following and this is evident from the size of the crowds present at the feeding of the five thousand and from the crowds that lined the streets as he made his final journey into Jerusalem shortly before his passion.

John 12:12: The next day the great crowd that had come for the Feast heard that Jesus was on his way to Jerusalem. They took palm branches and went out to meet him, shouting, "Hosanna! Blessed is he who comes in the name of the Lord! Blessed is the King of Israel."

The gospel narratives also indicate that there must have been a large number of people present at the site of the crucifixion and these included priests and elders, soldiers and the ordinary citizens of Jerusalem.

Mark 15:29: Those who passed by hurled insults at him, shaking their heads and saying, "So! You who are going to destroy the Temple and build it in three days, come down from the cross and save yourself!"

Matthew 27:41: In the same way the chief priests, the teachers of the law and the elders mocked Him.

Luke 23:36: The soldiers also came up and mocked Him.

With all these officials, soldiers and other people present it's inconceivable that the followers of Jesus could have removed him from the cross prior to his death. After all, a guard of four soldiers conducted the crucifixions and they weren't permitted to leave the site until the victim was confirmed to be dead.

Matthew 27:36: (referring to the soldiers) 'And sitting down, they kept watch over him there.'

The fact that they sat down indicates that the soldiers were expecting to be there for a long time and it's also evident from John's gospel that there were indeed four soldiers present.

John 19:23: 'When the soldiers crucified Jesus, they took his clothes, dividing them into four shares, one for each of them ….'

Pilate's writings to Caesar on the crucifixion clearly illustrate that Pilate knew that Jesus was dead and there's no evidence that the Jewish authorities had any reason to believe that Jesus had somehow survived the crucifixion.

Indeed the gospel accounts reveal that they went to Pilate asking for the grave to be made secure with a guard of soldiers and that Pilate gave his consent for this to be done.

Matthew 27:62: The next day, the one after Preparation Day, the chief priests and the Pharisees went to Pilate.

"Sir", they said, "we remember that while he was still alive that deceiver said, "After three days I will rise again."

So give the order for the tomb to be made secure until the third day. Otherwise, his disciples may come and steal the body and tell the people that he has been raised from the dead. This last deception will be worse than the first."

"Take a guard," Pilate answered, "Go, make the tomb as secure as you know how." So they went and made the tomb secure by putting a seal on the stone and posting the guard.

The behaviour of the apostles after the crucifixion also indicates that it was obvious to them that Jesus was dead as they went into mourning and locked themselves away in a safe house.

John 20:19: 'On the evening of that first day of the week, when the disciples were together, with the doors locked for fear of the Jews ….'

Also the writings of **Tacitus** in chapter 15 verse 44 of the **Annals** shows that Jesus had certainly died on the cross:

'The originator of that name, Christus, had been executed when Tiberius was Emperor, by order of the procurator Pontius Pilatus.'

Some have proposed that the disciples somehow managed to steal the body of Jesus from the tomb and others have even suggested that Jesus survived the crucifixion and lancing and was later able to escape from the tomb himself, but there are very obvious problems with these hypotheses.

How would the disciples have removed the body when there was a large detachment of Roman guards standing right outside the tomb? Also, none of the non-biblical historical writings record such an event as having happened.

In medical terms it's difficult to comprehend how anyone could have survived two prolonged beatings; a severe 'half death' flogging, crucifixion and then being lanced through the side, before being placed in a tomb.

The emergence of a sudden flow of blood and water as Jesus was lanced possibly indicates that the heart membrane had previously ruptured releasing accumulated fluid into the thoracic cavity and this would undoubtedly have resulted in death.

So all the evidence leads us to one conclusion and that is that Jesus certainly died on the cross at Calvary.

- Chapter 10 -
3rd piece of evidence: Inexplicable darkness and earthquake

Certain geological and astronomical events coincided with the crucifixion and death of Jesus and the first was a prolonged period of darkness in the middle of the day, during which it was so dark that the stars could be seen!

The second was a severe earthquake which struck Jerusalem on the afternoon of the crucifixion and which damaged the temple, tearing the 60 foot high curtain at the entrance to the Holy of Holies in two.

Matthew 27:45: 'From the sixth hour until the ninth hour darkness came over all the land.'

Luke 23:44: 'It was now about the sixth hour, and darkness came over the whole land until the ninth hour, for the sun stopped shining. And the curtain of the Temple was torn in two.'

Matthew 27:50: 'And when Jesus had cried out again in a loud voice, he gave up his spirit. At that moment the curtain of the temple was torn in two from top to bottom. The earth shook and the rocks split.'

From these accounts you would assume that there'd been a solar eclipse. However the crucifixion occurred at Passover time and the Passover is always celebrated at the time of a **full moon**, the first full moon after the vernal equinox.

A total solar eclipse, where the moon passes between the Earth and the Sun, thereby covering it, can only occur where there is a **new moon**, not a full moon.

Total solar eclipses are very rare events and the astronomers Russell, Dugan and Stewart in their classical textbook 'Astronomy' wrote:

'Since the track of a solar eclipse is a very narrow path over the earth's surface, averaging only 60 or 70 miles in width, we find that in the long run a total eclipse happens at any given station only once in about **360 years**.'

In addition to this, over a period of a thousand years there are usually fewer than ten eclipses that last for over seven minutes anywhere on the planet. But even these exceptional, prolonged total solar eclipses cannot possibly exceed **7 minutes and 31 seconds** which is the maximum time it can take for the Moon to pass over the sphere of the Sun!

However the records show that the darkness covered the land for a matter of hours and not seven minutes.

As there was a full moon at the time, some have suggested that it could have been a **lunar eclipse**, which occurs when the Moon passes behind the Earth and into its shadow i.e. the Earth is between the Sun and the Moon, with all three bodies aligned. In this situation the Earth's shadow blocks the light from the Sun which otherwise would reflect off the Moon.

A total lunar eclipse is where the Earth's shadow completely covers the Moon and this lasts for considerably longer than a Solar Eclipse. The Moon itself would be darkened and may sometimes appear reddish in colour due to the refracted light passing through dust in the atmosphere.

However the darkness caused by a total lunar eclipse is only present on the **night side of the planet** and Jerusalem at midday was quite clearly on the day side of the planet.

Now this darkness was not just described in the gospels, but was also mentioned by **Tertullian,** who clearly did not believe that the phenomenon was caused by an eclipse!

The Apologeticum, Chapter 21: 'In the same hour, too, the light of day was withdrawn, when the sun at the very time was in his meridian blaze. Those who were not aware that this had been predicted about Christ, no doubt thought it an eclipse. You yourselves have the account of the world-portent still in your archives.'

The Greek historian **Phlegon** also referred to the inexplicable darkness in his 'History of the Olympiads' written about 137 AD. He wrote:

'In the fourth year of the 202nd Olympiad, there was an eclipse of the Sun which was greater than any known before and in the sixth hour of the day it became night; so that stars appeared in the heaven; and a great Earthquake that broke out in Bithynia destroyed the greatest part of Nicaea.'

The fourth year of the 202nd Olympiad ran from July 32 AD through to the end of June 33 AD.

No explanation for the cause of this darkness has been provided by science, in the same way that no satisfactory explanation for the miracle of the Sun at Fatima on 13th October 1917 has been offered, despite the fact that it was witnessed by 70,000 people.

As the disciplines of astronomy and physics cannot explain the cause of this three hour period of darkness in the middle of the day, we must conclude that this was indeed a supernatural event.

The gospel writings also refer to an earthquake and the parochet or curtain hanging in the temple being torn in two. This massive blue, purple and scarlet coloured curtain is thought to have been sixty feet high and it was four inches thick.

The historian Josephus wrote that the curtain in the first temple (Solomon's temple) was 30 cubits high (about 45 feet) but that in the temple built by Herod it was extended to 40 cubits or about 60 feet high. Josephus also wrote that it was so heavy that horses tethered to each side could not pull the curtain apart.

The curtain was suspended from a huge lintel and it's likely that the earthquake damaged or displaced the lintel and the support pillars which would have resulted in the curtain being torn. However the timing of the event is absolutely extraordinary as Matthew recorded that it happened at the very moment Jesus died.

There was massive symbolism in this event and in the timing of it, because this curtain provided a barrier to the Holy of Holies where the Ark of the Covenant was placed and the Jews believed that the presence of God on earth existed here. The curtain showed that man was separated from God due to his sinfulness and only the High Priest could pass through the curtain to make atonement for their sins.

The implication of this curtain being ripped apart and so exposing the Holy of Holies is that all mankind can have their sins atoned through the sacrifice of Jesus and be worthy of entering the presence of God. Jesus in effect has become the new High Priest for all people who have faith in him and he alone can now make atonement for sins.

Regarding the inexplicable darkness, even if this had been caused by an eclipse, could it be a coincidence that an earthquake and an eclipse happened simultaneously at the exact time in history as the crucifixion of Jesus?

Possible, but how infinitely remote are the odds on this happening? In any event this total darkness lasted for a few hours in the middle of the day and could not have been caused by an eclipse.

As mentioned above, the great earthquake wasn't just described by the authors of the gospels, but was also recorded by the Greek historian Phlegon and there's also evidence in the geological record of earthquakes having struck Jerusalem in both 31 AD and in 33 AD.

The Dead Sea is extremely saline and therefore doesn't have organisms disturbing the sediment, which means that over geological time there's been an excellent preservation of the laminated clay and aragonite sedimentary layers.

Much analysis of the upper 6 metres of the sediments has been undertaken and this represents a period of around 4000 years of deposition. Earthquakes are easily identified in this geological record because they produce a band in the core samples in which the minerals are mixed (homogenous) instead of being separated into the usual distinctive strata.

There's also supporting evidence in sediment outcrops of the Wadi Ze'elim delta in the south western corner of the Dead Sea, where the distinctive silicated mud and aragonite layers are interrupted with homogenous areas produced by major seismic activity.

It's interesting that the geological record here also provides evidence of the major **Qumran earthquake** which struck in 31 BC and Josephus wrote that 30,000 men perished in it.

The gospels record an earthquake striking Jerusalem on the day of the crucifixion (Friday) and also on the day of the resurrection the following Sunday, so the second earthquake was clearly an aftershock.

The earthquake must have been a minimum of 5.5 on the Richter scale to have caused structural damage in Jerusalem and the destruction cited by Phlegon in his History of the Olympiads surely points to this having been a severe earthquake.

He wrote, 'and a great Earthquake that broke out in Bithynia destroyed the greatest part of Nicaea.' The damage caused was clearly widespread as the city of Nicaea is close to Istanbul in northwest Turkey and so about 1100 kilometres from Jerusalem. At the time of Jesus it was one of the most important cities in Asia Minor but it would again be devastated by earthquakes in 123 and 740 AD.

The coincidence of the inexplicable darkness and the earthquake occurring on the exact day in history that Jesus was crucified, surely provides food for thought for people who deny the divinity of Jesus.

Even if the darkness had been caused by a total solar eclipse then the chance of this happening on the very day that Jesus was crucified would be 1 in 360 years x 365.25 days = **1 in 131,490**.

There are estimated to have been 20 major earthquakes that have hit Jerusalem in the 1958 years from the Qumran earthquake of 31 BC to the 1927 Jericho earthquake that measured 6.3 on the Richter scale.

So this gives a probability of there being a major earthquake every 97.9 years. But the probability of one striking Jerusalem on the very day Jesus died would be 1 in 97.9 years x 365.25 days = **1 in 35,758**.

The probability of there being **both** a total solar eclipse and a major earthquake in Jerusalem on the very day of the crucifixion would therefore be 1 in 131,490 x 1 in 35,758 = **1 in 4.7 billion**!

The reaction of the pagan soldiers who had crucified Jesus and who were standing by his cross also show that the events that afternoon were absolutely breathtaking to witness.

Matthew 27:54: When the centurion and those with him who were guarding Jesus saw the earthquake and all that had happened, they were terrified, and exclaimed, "Surely he was the Son of God!"

Something indeed terrified these hardened soldiers, but only two years before there had been another earthquake, so it must have been more than this that terrified them. The reaction of the crowds was also one of complete shock.

Luke 23:48: 'When all the people who had gathered to witness this sight saw what took place, they beat their breasts and went away.'

These people had been hurling insults at Jesus as he was dying, so how do we explain this dramatic change in their behaviour in a matter of a few hours? The events must have been shattering to witness.

The high priests, elders and the Sanhedrin would have been very aware of the inexplicable darkness, the earthquake, the massive curtain in their temple being torn in two and the other phenomena. There would have been anger and confusion on the streets and even Pilate and his wife Claudia Procula went into fasting.

Shortly before the trial of Jesus the people had lined the streets of Jerusalem intent on proclaiming him as their King, but Caiaphas and the elders had acted quickly and ensured that Jesus was arrested and then tried in the early hours of the morning, while the vast majority of the citizens of Jerusalem were asleep.

During the trial before Pilate they had successfully stirred a large part of the crowd up into shouting for the execution of Jesus. However after the spectacular phenomena they had just witnessed at Calvary, the religious leaders would have felt the sea-change in emotions of the Jewish people.

They would certainly have seen the public beating of breasts by the crowds walking back to the city from Golgotha and realised that they were at real risk themselves from the people.

The prolonged darkness, for which there's no scientific explanation, and the coincidence of a major earthquake striking Jerusalem at the exact time in history as the crucifixion of Jesus, provides the third piece of evidence that he was divine.

- Chapter 11 -
4th piece of evidence: A guarded tomb found empty

The fears of the chief priests and elders had prompted them to ask Pilate to post a large 'guard' at the tomb of Jesus, as they realised that the presence of his corpse would certainly destroy any claims that he was divine.

At this time in Roman history, had the body of a deceased person been removed whilst under guard, or had a prisoner under guard escaped, all the guards would have faced execution.

Also a 'guard' at this time comprised multiple soldiers, generally at least four, as can be seen from the soldiers posted to watch Peter after his arrest by King Herod.

Acts 12:4: 'After arresting him, he put him in prison, handing him over to be guarded by four squads of four soldiers each.'

Pilate had very nearly faced a riot during the trial, so it was also in his best interest to ensure that this matter went away quickly and quietly. After all, this execution had touched everybody in the city including his own wife Claudia Procula, who had intervened during the trial and had attempted to prevent her husband from passing judgement on Jesus.

Matthew 27:19: While Pilate was sitting on the judge's seat his wife sent him this message: "Don't have anything to do with that innocent man, for I have suffered a great deal today in a dream because of him."

The chief priests had been given a mandate by Pilate to do whatever they could to make the tomb secure, so there was absolutely no excuse for them getting it wrong.

Now if Jesus didn't rise from the dead, then there's an obvious question to answer - what happened to his remains?

Also, if there was no resurrection how could the Christian movement have grown so rapidly?

If there had been a corpse to show, it would have been self evident to everyone living in Jerusalem that Jesus was not the Christ, yet the rapid spread of the early Church can be seen in **Acts 2:41**:

'Those who accepted his message were baptised and about three thousand were added to their number that day.'

The chief priests would obviously have seized on any opportunity to disprove the resurrection and if there was a body then surely they would have used this as evidence to show that Jesus was a fake. This would have stopped the movement in its tracks, so why did they not do this?

Josephus, who was born just four years after the crucifixion, was absolutely convinced that Jesus had indeed risen from the dead.

This is clear from his work 'The Antiquities' in a passage called the Testimonium Flavianum. (Book 18, chapter 3, verse 3)

'And when Pilate, because of an accusation made by the leading men among us, condemned him to the cross, those who had loved him previously did not cease to do so. **For he appeared to them on the third day, living again**, just as the divine prophets had spoken of these and countless other wondrous things about him.'

A comparative analysis of the four gospel accounts of the resurrection yields some fascinating information about what happened early on the Sunday morning.

Matthew 28:1: After the Sabbath, at dawn on the first day of the week, Mary Magdalene and the other Mary went to look at the tomb. There was a **violent earthquake**, for an angel of the Lord came down from heaven and, going to the tomb, rolled back the stone and sat on it. His appearance was like lightning, and his clothes were white as snow. **The guards were so afraid of him that they shook and became like dead men.**

The angel said to the women, "Do not be afraid, for I know that you are looking for Jesus, who was crucified. He is not here; he has risen, just as he said. Come and see the place where he lay. Then go quickly and tell his disciples: 'He has risen from the dead and is going ahead of you into Galilee. There you will see him.' Now I have told you." So the women hurried away from the tomb, afraid yet filled with joy, and ran to tell his disciples.

Suddenly Jesus met them. "Greetings," he said.

They came to him, clasped his feet and worshipped him. Then Jesus said to them, "Do not be afraid. Go and tell my brothers to go to Galilee; there they will see me."

Mark 16:1: When the Sabbath was over, Mary Magdalene, Mary the mother of James, and Salome bought spices so that they might go to anoint Jesus' body.

Very early on the first day of the week, just after sunrise, they were on their way to the tomb and they asked each other, "Who will roll the stone away from the entrance of the tomb?" But when they looked up, they saw that the stone, **which was very large**, had been rolled away.

As they entered the tomb, they saw a young man dressed in a white robe sitting on the right side, and they were alarmed.

"Don't be alarmed," he said. "You are looking for Jesus the Nazarene, who was crucified. He has risen! He is not here. See the place where they laid him.

"But go, tell his disciples and Peter, 'He is going ahead of you into Galilee. There you will see him, just as he told you.'"

Trembling and bewildered, the women went out and fled from the tomb. They said nothing to anyone, because they were afraid.

Luke 24:1: On the first day of the week, very early in the morning, the women took the spices they had prepared and went to the tomb. They found the stone rolled away from the tomb, but when they entered, they did not find the body of the Lord Jesus.

While they were wondering about this, suddenly two men in clothes that gleamed like lightning stood beside them. In their fright the women bowed down their faces to the ground, but the men said to them, "Why do you look for the living among the dead? He is not here; he has risen! Remember how he told you, while he was still with you in Galilee: The Son of Man must be delivered into the hands of sinful men, be crucified and on the third day be raised again." Then they remembered his words.

When they came back from the tomb, they told all these things to the Eleven and to all the others. It was Mary Magdalene, Joanna, Mary the mother of James, and the others with them who told this to the apostles.

But they did not believe the women, because their words seemed to them like nonsense. Peter, however, got up and ran to the tomb. Bending over, he saw the strips of linen lying by themselves, and he went away, wondering to himself what had happened.

Now John's account is unique in that he was writing in the third person, as he was 'the other disciple, the one Jesus loved.' John was present at the crucifixion and saw Jesus die and he and Peter were the only two apostles who actually went into the tomb according to the gospels.

John 20:1: Early on the first day of the week, while it was still dark, Mary Magdalene went to the tomb and saw that the stone had been removed from the entrance. So she came running to Simon Peter and the other disciple, the one Jesus loved, and said, "They have taken the Lord out of the tomb, and we don't know where they have put him!"

So Peter and the other disciple started for the tomb. Both were running, but the other disciple outran Peter and reached the tomb first. He bent over and looked in at the strips of linen lying there but did not go in.

Then Simon Peter, who was behind him, arrived and went into the tomb. He saw the strips of linen lying there, as well as the burial cloth that had been around Jesus' head. **The cloth was folded up by itself, separate from the linen**. Finally the other disciple, who had reached the tomb first, also went inside. He saw and believed.

Then the disciples went back to their homes, but Mary stood outside the tomb crying. As she wept, she bent over to look into the tomb and saw two angels in white, seated where Jesus' body had been, one at the head and the other at the foot.

They asked her, "Woman, why are you crying?"

"They have taken my Lord away," she said "and I don't know where they have put him."

At this she turned around and saw Jesus standing there, but she did not realise that it was Jesus.

"Woman," he said, "Why are you crying? Who is it you are looking for?"

Thinking he was the gardener, she said, "Sir, if you have carried him away, tell me where you have put him, and I will get him."

Jesus said to her, "Mary."

She turned towards him and cried out in Aramaic, "Rabboni!" (which means teacher).

Jesus said, "Do not hold on to me, for I have not yet returned to the Father. Go instead to my brothers and tell them, 'I am returning to my Father and your Father, to my God and your God."

Mary Magdalene went to the disciples with the news: "I have seen the Lord!" And she told them that he had said these things to her.

The earliest of the gospels was written a minimum of thirty years after the death of Jesus and so it's understandable that there'll be some slight variations in emphasis and detail.

For example Matthew mentions the second earthquake but the other writers omit this and all the gospel writers refer to two or more women having visited the tomb, except for John, who only mentions Mary Magdalene.

From the text in John it reads as though Mary, after having initially reported the news to the disciples, must have returned to the tomb with Peter and John a second time.

John arrived first as he was only about twenty seven years old and probably quite fit, followed by Peter himself and so Mary Magdalene may have arrived shortly after Peter.

She was still there after Peter and John had left and so it's understandable that John would put the emphasis on Mary in his account. The women went to the tomb very early on the Sunday morning and this was probably so that they wouldn't be seen and reported to the chief priests.

The rock at the entrance of the tomb is a key point mentioned in all four writings, with Mark noting that it was 'very large.'

An angel or angels (men in white) are referred to in all four accounts but the terrified guards are only mentioned by Matthew and this is important as it shows that the guards were still there on the Sunday

111

morning and that the tomb had not been left unguarded, as per Pilate's instructions.

The strips of linen were only mentioned by Luke and John, with the latter giving a more detailed description. John wrote that the burial cloth which had been around Jesus' head was folded up by itself. This is another important detail as it surely implies that whoever removed the linen and burial cloth was in no hurry, as they had time to fold it up!

It also raises the question as to why the burial linen was removed from the body at all!

If some party intended to steal the body of Jesus, why wouldn't they just have removed it with the burial cloth still on?

If we propose that the body was indeed stolen, then those who took it must surely have been under pressure in terms of the time they had available to do this without being detected.

It's surely illogical that they would waste a lot of time and take the risk of being caught in order to unwrap the body and to fold the head cloth up separately.

Two of the accounts show the women running away from the grave to the disciples and John's account has Mary Magdalene rushing to give the news of the empty tomb only to himself and Peter.

However after she'd returned to the site and encountered Jesus outside the grave, she then went to the disciples with the news. Matthew and John both record an encounter between the women and Jesus near the tomb.

Now we get a brief description of the tomb itself in **Matthew 27:57**:

'As evening approached, there came a rich man from Arimathea, named Joseph, who had himself become a disciple of Jesus. Going to Pilate he asked for Jesus' body, and Pilate ordered that it be given to him. Joseph took the body, wrapped it in a clean linen cloth, and placed it in his own new tomb that he had cut out of the rock. He rolled a big stone in front of the entrance to the tomb and went away.'

And from John's account we know that the grave was close to the actual site of the crucifixion.

John 19:41: 'At the place where Jesus was crucified, there was a garden, and in the garden a new tomb, in which no one had ever been laid. Because it was the Jewish day of Preparation and since the tomb was near by, they laid Jesus there.'

The grave itself must have been large enough to accommodate a corpse and at least two people, but possibly three. This is clear from Mark's account as Mary Magdalene and Mary the mother of James both went into the tomb where they saw a young man already sitting inside the grave on the right side.

John's account also depicts both Peter and John being in the grave together and it follows that the rock that was rolled in front of the entrance must have been very heavy due to the size of the opening it had to cover!

The entrance to the tomb was clearly below head height as John records that he bent over to look into the tomb and he also describes Mary as having to do the same.

It's possible that there was an incline to make it easier to roll the rock into place and this would also ensure the rock had a closer fit against the opening. However if there was an incline it would have made it far more difficult to move the rock away from the grave than it was to roll the rock towards it.

In any event, to move a massive rock away from the entrance to a tomb like this would no doubt require the strength of several men.

The chief priests were now confronted with news that must have been absolutely devastating to them. **Matthew 28:11**:

'While the women were on their way, some of the guards went into the city and reported to the chief priests everything that had happened. When the chief priests had met with the elders and devised a plan, they gave the soldiers a large sum of money, telling them, "you are to say, 'His disciples came during the night and stole him away while we were asleep.' If this report gets to the governor, we will satisfy him and keep you out of trouble." So the soldiers took the money and did as they were instructed. And this story has been widely circulated among the Jews to this very day.'

It's clear that the soldiers went straight from the grave site to the chief priests with the news about the angel and the empty tomb and this seems perfectly logical as they would have risked being put to death if they'd gone to Pilate with this news.

The chief priests were therefore confronted with two stark possibilities - either the soldiers were lying, or Jesus had indeed risen from death.

They knew full well that if Jesus had risen from the dead that this would prove that he was the Son of God, because he'd given this as the acid test of his divinity long before he died. If the masses found out about this, then they would surely turn on the chief priests and elders of the Sanhedrin.

But at this time there'd been no sightings or reports of a risen Jesus apart from what the soldiers had told them and so they may still have had some doubts that he had actually risen from death.

However this would imply that the soldiers were all lying and the chief priests would have been unable to think of a reasonable motivation for them doing such a thing.

Also they would have been able to tell from the behaviour of the guards that they'd indeed witnessed something deeply shocking. Matthew even wrote that the guards had been so afraid of the angel that they shook and became like dead men.

So the chief priests decided to bribe the soldiers in order to keep these startling revelations to themselves. Of course they were no strangers to bribery and money from the temple coffers had previously been used by them to entice Judas to betray Jesus in the first place.

These priests were the same people who had planned to kill Lazarus, a man that had been raised from the dead and the priests had also made false accusations at the trial of Jesus to have him put to death.

So out of the Ten Commandments that they preached with such zeal, they were quite prepared to break at least three of them - bearing false witness, stealing and murder and they would clearly have stopped at nothing to keep the resurrection quiet!

But what's clear from the texts is that on the Sunday morning the tomb was certainly empty and there are various possible explanations for this which we need to examine.

Was Jesus never buried after being taken down from the cross?

Joseph of Arimathea had asked Pilate for permission to remove the body from the cross and to bury it and Pilate had subsequently asked for confirmation from the centurion that Jesus was in fact dead, before granting this request. The soldiers are likely to have watched Joseph and Nicodemus take the body down and may even have assisted them in removing the nails.

Now there would still have been soldiers and large numbers of people in the area at that time of day and it's likely that there were elders observing Joseph and Nicodemus as well, because they were suspicious that the disciples would try and steal the body.

It's therefore highly unlikely that they would have attempted to remove the body and carry it away instead of burying it. But even if this was feasible, what possible motive would there have been for them to have done this?

Was the body removed from the grave before the guards arrived?

This is a more plausible hypothesis than the one above. Matthew wrote that the chief priests and the Pharisees went to Pilate the next day i.e. the day after the crucifixion, to ask for his permission to post a guard.

So unless the chief priests organised a guard themselves, there was no-one guarding the tomb from when Jesus was buried late afternoon or early evening Friday until sometime on the Saturday.

However, it's difficult to imagine that the chief priests wouldn't have recognised this possibility and ensured that the tomb was supervised through Friday night into Saturday morning, by Jewish soldiers from their own Temple Guard.

But even if it was unguarded for this period, what possible motivation would there have been for removing the body? Where would they have taken it?

The disciples would have been imprisoned or possibly even executed had they been caught stealing the body in the middle of the night. Also, it would have taken several men to remove the rock and they would have required long wooden poles to use for leverage, as well as lamps to see what they were doing and all this activity would easily have been detected.

Even if they did manage to remove the body and then dispose of it somewhere, why would they all have given up their lives preaching that Jesus was the Messiah if they knew this to be patently untrue?

Also, when the Roman guards arrived the next morning to seal the stone, they would have seen that it had been displaced and that the tomb was empty and reported it, but this didn't happen.

Were the women and the apostles looking at the wrong grave?

Now in his gospel, Luke describes the women as having gone with Joseph of Arimathea to the grave site near Calvary.

Luke 23:55: 'The women who had come with Jesus from Galilee followed Joseph and saw the tomb and how his body was laid in it.'

So the women knew the precise location of the grave site and even if they had mistakenly gone to the wrong grave initially, then Joseph and Nicodemus would surely have corrected them later.

It also seems improbable that Joseph would have made this mistake, as it was his own tomb which he'd hewn out of the rock himself.

Did the chief priests have the body removed?

This would have been possible, as they could have bribed the guards to allow them to remove the body or even had permission from Pilate to remove the corpse. However for this to be plausible we would need a motive.

One motive could be that they took the body so as to keep it secure and to prevent any attempt by the disciples to steal it. But for this to make sense they must surely have intended putting it back on day four or later, to prove to the people that Jesus hadn't risen from the dead.

Clearly by removing the corpse and never putting it back they would be playing into the hands of the disciples, as it would have provided evidence that Jesus had indeed risen from the dead.

So if we propose that the chief priests and elders initially took the body, why didn't they put it back later?

Also if this was their plan all along, then why did they go to Pilate requesting a guard in the first place? So this hypothesis doesn't stand up to scrutiny either.

Is it possible that Pilate ordered the removal of the corpse?

He certainly had the capacity to do this, but what would his motive have been? By removing the corpse the Jews would be more inclined to believe that Jesus was the Christ and so Pilate would then have risked civil unrest, as it was he that had ordered him to be put to death.

As Pilate had passed the death sentence to prevent rioting on the streets, it seems illogical that he would then have risked massive unrest by removing the body of Jesus.

Again, what would the motive have been for him to do this?

Did the disciples take the body while it was under guard?

This was the explanation that the chief priests conceived. But in order to have stolen the body, the disciples would have had to have bribed the guards or else distracted them away from the grave site, or found a way of drugging them.

But we need to remember that these disciples are the same men who had fled the garden of Gethsemane when Jesus was arrested and Peter had even denied knowing Jesus three times when he was being questioned by Caiaphas and the Sanhedrin.

Apart from John, Mary the mother of Jesus and the other women, the disciples are not recorded as having been near the cross of Jesus as he was dying. They'd all gone into hiding for fear of being arrested, so it's difficult to comprehend how they suddenly gained the courage to attempt the removal of the body from a well guarded grave.

Tertullian wrote in chapter 21 of his work 'Apologeticum' that it was a 'large military guard' and so it may well have comprised more than 4 soldiers.

"Then, when His body was taken down from the cross and placed in a sepulchre, the Jews in their eager watchfulness surrounded it with a large military guard, lest, as He had predicted His resurrection from the dead on the third day, His disciples might remove by stealth His body, and deceive even the incredulous."

It's quite inconceivable that all the guards would have fallen asleep simultaneously and if they were all drugged, then surely they would have informed Pilate or the chief priests about this after they'd recovered from the effect of the drugs.

Also, what would the motive have been for the disciples to have stolen the body and why would they all have been willing to die later for a cause that they knew to be a complete hoax?

None of the above hypotheses would explain the behaviour of the guards, the sighting of an angel or the subsequent actions of the disciples.

So then how do we explain the empty tomb?

The only remaining possibility is that Jesus had indeed miraculously risen from the dead, as he had himself raised Lazarus from death.

When viewed in this light, then the behaviour of the guards and the actions of the chief priests is entirely logical and so is the reaction of the women and the apostles after the resurrection.

So the empty grave on the Sunday morning is the fourth piece of evidence that points to Jesus having been divine.

- Chapter 12 -
5th piece of evidence: Post resurrection appearances

Matthew wrote that Jesus first appeared to both Mary Magdalene and Mary the mother of James and Joses outside the tomb, whereas Mark and John's gospels have Jesus first appearing to Mary Magdalene alone.

Luke on the other hand gives the account of Jesus appearing to a man named Cleopas and his friend who were walking the eleven kilometres from Jerusalem to Emmaus, but implies that Jesus had already appeared to Simon Peter earlier in the day.

Luke 24:28: As they approached the village to which they were going, Jesus acted as if he were going further. But they urged him strongly, "Stay with us for it is nearly evening; the day is almost over."

So he went in to stay with them. When he was at the table with them, he took bread, gave thanks, broke it and began to give it to them. Then their eyes were opened and they recognised him, and he disappeared from their sight.

They asked each other "Were not our hearts burning within us while he talked with us on the road and opened the Scriptures to us?"

Then they got up and returned at once to Jerusalem. There they found the Eleven and those with them, assembled together and saying, "It is true! The Lord has risen and has appeared to Simon."

Then the two told what had happened on the way, and how Jesus was recognised by them when he broke the bread.

While they were still talking about this, Jesus himself stood among them and said to them, "Peace be with you."

They were startled and frightened, thinking they saw a ghost. He said to them, "Why are you troubled, and why do doubts rise in your minds? Look at my hands and my feet. It is I myself! Touch me and see; a ghost does not have flesh and bones, as you see I have."

When he had said this, he showed them his hands and feet. And while they still did not believe it because of joy and amazement, he asked them, "Do you have anything here to eat?" They gave him a piece of broiled fish, and he took it and ate it in their presence.

John 20:24: Now Thomas, one of the Twelve, was not with the disciples when Jesus came. So the other disciples told him, "We have seen the Lord!"

But he said to them, "Unless I see the nail marks in his hands and put my finger where the nails were, and put my hand into his side, I will not believe it."

A week later his disciples were in the house again, and Thomas was with them. Though the doors were locked, Jesus came and stood among them, and said, "Peace be with you!"

Then he said to Thomas, "Put your finger here; see my hands. Reach out your hand and put it into my side. Stop doubting and believe."

Thomas answered, "My Lord and my God!"

Then Jesus told him, "Because you have seen me, you have believed; blessed are those who have not seen and yet have believed."

Jesus did many other miraculous signs in the presence of his disciples, which are not recorded in this book. But these are written that you may believe that Jesus is the Christ, the Son of God, and that by believing you may have life in his name.

John 21:1 Afterwards Jesus appeared again to his disciples, by the Sea of Tiberias. It happened this way: Simon Peter, Thomas (called Didymus), Nathanael from Cana in Galilee, the sons of Zebedee, and two other disciples were together.

"I'm going out to fish," Simon Peter told them, and they said, "We'll go with you." So they went out and got into the boat, but that night they caught nothing.

Early in the morning, Jesus stood on the shore, but the disciples did not realise that it was Jesus.

He called out to them, "Friends, haven't you any fish?"

"No," they answered.

He said, "Throw your net on the right side of the boat and you will find some."

When they did, they were unable to haul the net in because of the large number of fish. Then the disciple whom Jesus loved said to Peter, "It is the Lord!"

As soon as Simon Peter heard him say, "It is the Lord," he wrapped his outer garment around him (for he had taken it off) and jumped into the water. The other disciples followed in the boat, towing the net full of fish, for they were not far from shore, about ninety metres. When they landed they saw a fire of burning coals there with fish on it, and some bread.

Jesus said to them, "Bring some of the fish you have just caught."

Simon Peter climbed aboard and dragged the net ashore. It was full of large fish, 153, but even with so many the net was not torn.

Jesus said to them, "Come and have breakfast."

Now Paul also wrote something interesting about the post resurrection appearances of Jesus in his first letter to the Corinthians.

'For what I received I passed on to you as of first importance: that Christ died for our sins according to the Scriptures, and that he appeared to Peter, and then to the Twelve. After that, he appeared to **more than five hundred** of the brothers at the same time, most of whom are still living, though some have fallen asleep. Then he appeared to James, then to all the apostles, and last of all he appeared to me also, as to one abnormally born.' (**1 Corinthians 15:3**)

This passage is remarkable as it recounts Jesus appearing to over five hundred witnesses gathered together in the same place. It's also interesting that Jesus is recorded as having eaten with the disciples on a few occasions after his resurrection and from these accounts it can be seen that the resurrected Jesus had a physical presence and was not just spirit.

When Jesus drove the corrupt money lenders and traders out of the temple of Jerusalem, the furious elders had demanded a miraculous sign from him to prove who he was.

John 2:18: Then the Jews demanded of him, "What miraculous sign can you show us to prove your authority to do all this?"

Jesus answered them, "Destroy this temple, and I will raise it again in three days."

The Jews replied, "It has taken forty-six years to build this temple, and you are going to raise it in three days?" But the temple he had spoken off was his body. After he was raised from the dead, his disciples recalled what he had said. Then they believed the Scripture and the words that Jesus had spoken.

So by the words of Jesus himself, the resurrection would be the acid test of his claim to be divine. Of all the billions of people who have died throughout history, none has been able to regain life after being dead for a few days, with the exception of Lazarus, whom Jesus raised from the dead.

Now if Jesus hadn't risen from the dead, then he would still have been regarded as a prophet by many. After all, countless people had been cured by him after years of suffering, when the medical practitioners of the day had been unable to do so. In fact at his trial several of the people he'd cured bravely spoke out in his defence such as Bernice, when others remained silent.

Nine thousand men and probably at least three times that number counting women and children had watched a miracle unfold before their eyes at the feeding of the five thousand and the feeding of the four thousand.

Many had witnessed the raising of Lazarus from death after spending four days in a grave and others would have watched in amazement as Jesus brought the daughter of Jairus, a synagogue ruler back to life. Others would have seen him bring the son of a widow back from the dead in the town of Nain.

To be healed of an incurable disease would be a life-changing experience for anyone and the crowds watching these miracles would have been left absolutely stunned by what they saw.

So if the body of Jesus had still been in the grave, it would by necessity have become a site of pilgrimage. So why is this not mentioned in the writings of Josephus or Tacitus?

The answer is surely because there were no remains in the grave!

The church of the Holy Sepulchre in the old walled city of Jerusalem is believed to be the site of Golgotha where Jesus was crucified. Eusebius wrote that the original site had been covered with earth on Hadrian's instruction due to his hatred of Christians and that he subsequently had the temple of Aphrodite built on the site.

But in 325 AD, the emperor Constantine ordered that Aphrodite's temple be demolished and a church built there in its place and it was during the ground clearance that an empty tomb cut out of rock was found, which they believed to be the tomb of Jesus.

Constantine built two churches and a grand Basilica and the buildings connected the site of the crucifixion and the site of the tomb and they were linked by a long colonnade.

The church had a turbulent history and was destroyed in 1009 during a campaign against Christian places of worship in Palestine and only two pillars of the original structure survived.

However the Byzantine emperor Constantine Monomachus had the church rebuilt with five chapels and an open court and these were constructed on the site by around 1048 AD.

Within the complex is the 'Rock of Calvary' which is believed to be the actual rock through which the cross was erected. The 'Stone of Anointing' is also located in this church, which is thought to be where Joseph of Arimathea and Nicodemus prepared the body of Jesus for burial.

On the site is the Most Holy Sepulchre, which is believed to be the actual tomb of Jesus and 'The Angel's Stone' which is part of the rock that was used to seal the entrance to the tomb.

John refers to the garden where Jesus was buried as being at the place where he was crucified and it makes sense that the burial site was close to the site of the crucifixion, as it would have been difficult to carry the body of Jesus and 34 kilograms of myrrh and aloes for any great distance.

John 19:38: 'Later, Joseph of Arimathea asked Pilate for the body of Jesus. Now Joseph was a disciple of Jesus, but secretly because he feared the Jews. With Pilate's permission, he came and took the body away. He was accompanied by Nicodemus, the man who earlier had visited Jesus at night. Nicodemus brought a mixture of myrrh and aloes, about thirty-four kilograms.

Taking Jesus' body, the two of them wrapped it, with the spices, in strips of linen. This was in accordance with Jewish burial customs. At the place where Jesus was crucified, there was a garden, and in the garden a new tomb, in which no one had ever been laid. Because it was the Jewish day of Preparation and since the tomb was near by, they laid Jesus there.'

What's significant is that at no time in history has there been any indication that believers thought that there were the remains of Jesus in this tomb or at any other site.

The tombs of many of the apostles can be visited to this day, but the difference is that these tombs contain physical remains.

So the post resurrection appearances of Jesus provide the fifth piece of evidence that he was divine.

- Chapter 13 -
6th piece of evidence: Disciples prepared for martyrdom

In terms of psychology, what could possibly have motivated the apostles to spend the rest of their lives preaching that Jesus had risen from the dead?

After all, this was an undertaking that caused these young men the most incredible difficulties and that led almost all of them to their deaths by execution. It's surely illogical for them to have done this if they knew that the resurrection had never happened.

In the confusion of Gethsemane, the disciples had abandoned Jesus and run away from the garden, although one man seems to have continued following Jesus a bit further (possibly Mark) but was seized and only just managed to escape, running away naked.

Peter had denied his association with Jesus three times while he was being questioned by the chief priests and not one of the apostles defended Jesus either at his trial before Caiaphas or before Pontius Pilate. Immediately after his crucifixion, the disciples were clearly confused and far too frightened to walk out in public.

However according to Acts, there was a dramatic change in their behaviour at Pentecost, fifty days after the resurrection and the apostles came out of hiding and began preaching without fear in the streets of Jerusalem that Jesus was the Christ.

This behavioural change over such a short period of time defies logic and clearly something dramatic must have happened between the crucifixion and Pentecost.

According to Acts, Jesus appeared to the apostles and other disciples for a period of forty days and gave **convincing evidence** that he was alive. Now this experience would have been life changing to anyone witnessing it, as any doubt as to the divinity of Jesus would have evaporated.

In addition to this, his promise that he would raise believers in him to everlasting life, would have given the apostles enormous confidence and would explain their sudden loss of fear of the priests and elders.

Acts 1:3: After his suffering, he showed himself to these men and gave many convincing proofs that he was alive. He appeared to them over a period of forty days and spoke about the kingdom of God.

On one occasion, while he was eating with them, he gave them this command: "Do not leave Jerusalem, but wait for the gift my Father has promised, which you have heard me speak about. For John baptised with water, but in a few days you will be baptised with the Holy Spirit."

According to Luke, who wrote the Acts of the Apostles, the last time the apostles saw Jesus was when he was taken up into the sky forty days after the resurrection.

Acts 1:6: So when they met together, they asked him, "Lord, are you at this time going to restore the kingdom to Israel?"

He said to them, "It is not for you to know the times or dates the Father has set by his own authority. But you will receive power when the Holy Spirit comes on you; and you will be my witnesses in Jerusalem, and in all Judea and Samaria, and to the ends of the earth." After he said this, he was taken up before their very eyes, and a cloud hid him from their sight."

They were looking intently up into the sky as he was going, when suddenly two men dressed in white stood beside them. "Men of Galilee," they said, "Why do you stand here looking into the sky? This same Jesus, who has been taken from you into heaven, will come back in the same way you have seen him go into heaven."

Acts goes on to describe what happened at Pentecost which was fifty days after the resurrection and ten days after the apostles had witnessed the ascension.

Acts 2:1: When the day of Pentecost came, they were all together in one place. Suddenly a sound like the blowing of a violent wind came from heaven and filled the whole house where they were sitting. They saw what seemed to be tongues of fire that separated and came to rest on each of them. All of them were filled with the Holy Spirit and began to speak in other tongues as the Spirit enabled them.

Now there were staying in Jerusalem God-fearing Jews from every nation under heaven. When they heard this sound, a crowd came together in bewilderment, because each one heard them speaking in his own language.

Utterly amazed, they asked: "Are not all these men who are speaking Galileans? Then how is it that each of us hears them in his own native language?"

Acts continues with Peter standing up to tell the crowds that Jesus had risen from the dead and saying that they should all repent and be baptised.

This speech had clearly not been prepared in advance and yet it was noticeably eloquent and well structured for an uneducated fisherman. This is the same Peter who denied knowing Jesus in the courtyard of the house of the High Priest and the same man who was not at the crucifixion and the very person who'd been hiding behind a locked door for fear of the Jews.

So how do we explain this in terms of psychology? What had radically transformed his behaviour?

Not long after this, Peter is recorded as having healed a crippled beggar outside the Jerusalem temple gate in the name of Jesus. He and John were immediately arrested and brought before the Sanhedrin, where Peter once again showed uncharacteristic courage.

Acts 4:8: Then Peter, filled with the Holy Spirit, said to them: "Rulers and elders of the people! If we are being called to account today for an act of kindness shown to a man who was lame and are being asked how he was healed, then know this, you and all the people of Israel: It is by the name of Jesus Christ of Nazareth, whom you crucified but whom God raised from the dead, that this man stands before you healed.

Jesus is 'the stone you builders rejected, which has become the cornerstone.' Salvation is found in no one else, for there is no other name under heaven given to mankind by which we must be saved."

When they saw the courage of Peter and John and realised that they were unschooled, ordinary men, they were astonished and they took note that these men had been with Jesus. But since they could see the man who had been healed standing there with them, there was nothing they could say. So they ordered them to withdraw from the Sanhedrin and then conferred together.

"What are we going to do with these men?" they asked. "Everyone living in Jerusalem knows they have performed a notable sign, and we cannot deny it. But to stop this thing from spreading any further among the people, we must warn them to speak no longer to anyone in this name."

Then they called them in again and commanded them not to speak or teach at all in the name of Jesus. But Peter and John replied, "Which is right in God's eyes: to listen to you, or to him? You be the judges! As for us, we cannot help speaking about what we have seen and heard."

Notice how the chief priests didn't contest what Peter had said regarding Jesus being raised from the dead and also that they didn't accuse the apostles of having stolen the body!

The only explanation for this is that they knew full well that the tomb had inexplicably been found empty on the Sunday morning.

Again, notice how the elders of the Sanhedrin were unconcerned about the truth, but instead they were just determined to prevent news of the resurrection from reaching the people.

It would clearly have taken a radical experience to bring about a change in the behaviour of the apostles like this. When they met the risen Jesus for the first time in the upper room, they must have been utterly shocked, even though Jesus had often said that he would be raised to life on the third day.

They'd all seen the miracles that Jesus had worked and had watched him feed thousands of people with just a few loaves of bread and a couple of fish. They'd also witnessed Jesus raise Lazarus from the dead and Peter, James and John had even witnessed the magnificence of his transfiguration.

They'd all been immersed in a three hour period of total darkness in the middle of the day and had felt the devastating earthquake on the day of the crucifixion. Yet despite all these supernatural events, there were still doubts clouding their minds.

Luke wrote that when the women ran to the apostles and said that the grave was empty and that two angels had said that Jesus had risen from the dead, their words 'seemed like nonsense to them.'

Thomas still doubted even after all the other apostles and presumably Mary the mother of Jesus, Mary Magdalene and the other disciples had been telling him for a whole week that they'd seen Jesus.

The fact that the risen Jesus had a physical form and was eating with them must have been astonishing to the apostles and it's doubtful that they'd anticipated the physical reality of the resurrected Jesus.

Over the next forty days their understanding of what resurrection meant would have grown and they would have understood the reality that one day their own bodies would be raised from the dead and that there really was an after-life that was eternal.

The next shock would have been Jesus being taken up into the sky in front of them outside the town of Bethany and Jesus had yet again done something that was physically impossible.

He'd demonstrated his power over nature and life itself many times during his ministry, by raising the dead, walking on water and by calming a storm while he was out on a lake with the apostles. Now the resurrected Jesus was again seen to have power over the elements of nature.

The next life changing event was what happened in the upper room at Pentecost, where a violent wind and tongues of fire appeared, before separating and coming to rest on each of their heads.

The physical feeling they experienced at the moment the tongues of fire contacted their bodies was not recorded, but the reality was an instantaneous change in their capacity to communicate. They also became courageous when they'd been fearful before, as is evidenced by Peter immediately leaving the room to address the crowd.

These events changed the context of death for them and physical death was no longer something to be feared. In fact it was a release into an eternal life, an incomparably better existence with Jesus and this can be seen in Peter's defiance in front of the Sanhedrin, as he knew that by dying for Jesus he would be guaranteed eternal life.

Paul expressed this well in **Philippians 1:22**: 'If I am to go on living in the body, this will mean fruitful labour for me. Yet what shall I choose? I do not know! I am torn between the two: I desire to depart and be with Christ, which is better by far; but it is more necessary for you that I remain in the body.'

Most of the apostles were martyred for preaching that Jesus was the Messiah and a very brief description of their lives shows just how much they suffered in his name.

Simon had been given the name Cephas by Jesus which means rock or stone in the Aramaic language and the Greek equivalent of this is Petros. In his gospel, Matthew records the conversation in which Jesus gave Peter a leadership role.

Matthew 16:15: "But what about you?" he asked. "Who do you say I am?"

Simon Peter answered, "You are the Christ, the Son of the living God."

Jesus replied, "Blessed are you, Simon son of Jonah, for this was not revealed to you by man, but by my Father in heaven. And I tell you that you are Peter, and on this rock I will build my church, and the gates of Hades will not overcome it. I will give you the keys of the kingdom of heaven; whatever you bind on earth will be bound in heaven, and whatever you loose on earth will be loosed in heaven."

Peter was arrested during the persecution of the church by Herod Agrippa in 44 AD, immediately after James had been executed and although shackled at the wrists and guarded by four soldiers, he miraculously escaped from prison.

He preached in Antioch for some time and built the first Christian church there and it was here that the disciples were first named 'Christians.'

Peter's leadership was evident at the council of Jerusalem, where there was a heated debate about whether Gentiles had to be circumcised or not. It was Peter who stood up and addressed the apostles and elders and who made the pronouncement that circumcision wasn't a requirement for Gentiles.

Peter may have travelled in Asia Minor, but he spent most of his ministry in Rome, possibly as long as twenty-five years, with Mark acting as his interpreter there for some time.

It's thought that the Emperor Nero had him imprisoned in the infamous Mamertine Prison in Rome for nine months, shackled and kept in total darkness.

He was later crucified and although the date of his death is uncertain, it was probably around 67-68 AD in the middle of the Jewish Roman war.

In his writings, Origen stated that 'Peter was crucified at Rome with his head downwards, as he himself had desired to suffer.'

Eusebius wrote that both Peter and Paul were executed in the thirteenth or fourteenth year of Nero, which supports the 67-68 AD date.

James (also called James the greater) was the brother of John and was also a fisherman. He, along with Peter and John were the only apostles to witness the transfiguration of Jesus and in the Garden of Gethsemane Jesus took Peter, James and John with him deeper into the garden to pray. These three were also the only apostles present when the daughter of Jairus was raised to life.

James preached in his home town of Bethsaida where he had a church built, but tradition has it that he also preached in Spain, as there's a strong association with the town of Compostela.

What's certain is that he was the first apostle to be martyred and he was beheaded in Judea on the instruction of King Herod Agrippa in 44 AD. According to Clement of Alexandria, the man who brought the case against James repented and then converted to Christianity, before being beheaded with James. Agrippa, the grandson of Herod the Great, died that same year.

John was only about twenty four years of age when Jesus started his ministry and what makes him unique is that he was the only apostle known to have been present at the crucifixion.

Along with Peter, he was one of only two apostles to have entered the tomb of Jesus and John was often referred to as 'the disciple whom Jesus loved.'

The gospels record that Jesus spoke to John and to his mother from the cross at Calvary.

John 19:25: When Jesus saw his mother there, and the disciple whom he loved standing near by, he said to his mother, "Dear woman, here is your son," and to the disciple, "Here is your mother." From that time on, this disciple took her into his home.

It's thought that John preached in Judea for about twelve years but that he finally settled in Ephesus and there's a strong tradition that he built a house for Mary there.

Tertullian wrote in 'The prescription of Heretics' that John was arrested and taken to Rome during the reign of the Emperor Domitian, where an attempt was made to execute him by having him poisoned and then thrown into a cauldron of boiling oil.

When he miraculously emerged unhurt, the entire Colosseum was apparently converted. Domitian then banished him to the penal island of Patmos, but he returned to Ephesus a year later and built a church there and his was the last of the gospels to be written.

There's much controversy over whether it was he or another John (John of Patmos) who wrote the Book of Revelation. In his final years, John taught Polycarp who later became the bishop of Smyrna and John is thought to have died around 100 AD when he was about 94 years of age and he was buried at Selcuk near Ephesus.

Andrew preached in Cyprus, Greece and Turkey as well as present day Ukraine, southern Russia and Romania and he had a church built in Byzantium, which was later named Constantinople.

It's believed that he was martyred in Patras in Greece by being tied to an X shaped cross and that during the two days that it took him to die he continued preaching to those who gathered around him. His remains were originally preserved at Patras, but they were later transferred to Byzantium around 357 AD.

Over time, some of the relics found their way to the Vatican, but in 1964, Pope Paul VI sent the relics back to the Church of St Andrew in Patras.

Philip preached in Greece, Turkey and Syria and it's thought that he was martyred in Hierapolis, north west of Antalya in Turkey. Tradition has it that the wife of the Proconsul of Hierapolis listened to his preaching and also watched him perform a miraculous healing. She then converted to Christianity, which angered the Proconsul who then ordered his execution.

It's thought that he was crucified upside down and according to tradition Philip also continued to preach from his cross until he died. His relics are in the crypt of the Basilica Santi Apostoli in Rome.

Bartholomew (Nathanael) preached in Armenia, to the west of the Caspian Sea, but he also spread the gospel in Turkey with Philip and it's believed that he also taught in Iraq and Iran. What's intriguing is that both the historian Eusebius of Caesarea (263-339 AD) and Saint Jerome (347-420 AD) wrote that Bartholomew also preached in India.

Eusebius wrote that he left a Hebrew copy of Matthew's gospel in India and some scholars believe that he visited the ancient city of Kalyan, near present day Mumbai.

One tradition is that Bartholomew was martyred at Albanopolis in Armenia after having converted Polymius, the King of Armenia, to Christianity. Astyages, the King's brother had him executed because of this, by being skinned alive and then beheaded.

Matthew collected taxes, probably from the Jews for Herod Antipas, before becoming an apostle and he may well have known Zacchaeus the chief tax collector mentioned in the gospels. Tax collectors had to have a good understanding of both the Greek and Aramaic languages but they were highly unpopular people at the time of Jesus.

St Clement of Alexandria claimed that he taught among the Hebrews for fifteen years and he may have only left Judea during the persecution of the church by Herod Agrippa in 44 AD.

There's a tradition that he later preached in Ethiopia (not the Ethiopia in Africa but the area south of the Caspian Sea in Iran) but he may also have taught in Macedonia and Syria. Matthew wrote the first of the gospels and is thought to have been martyred, but exactly how he died is unclear.

Thomas is remembered for being the apostle who refused to accept the resurrection until he saw Jesus himself eight days later. However he showed great loyalty to Jesus during his ministry, such as the time Jesus suggested going back to Judea after Lazarus had died, where the Jews had recently tried to stone him. It was Thomas who said to the others, "Let us all go, that we may die with him."

It's thought that he preached in Iran and that he also evangelised in India, travelling as far south as Mylapore (Chennai) and there's a tradition that he was martyred in Chennai by being speared to death by four soldiers.

Some of his relics can be found at the San Thome Basilica in Chennai, although his skull is believed to be housed in the Monastery of Saint John the Theologian on the Greek island of Patmos. More of his relics are preserved in the Cathedral of St Thomas the Apostle in Ortona, Italy.

James, the son of Alphaeus (James the Less) is believed to have preached in Judea and Gaza and possibly also in Egypt and Syria as well. His mother Mary and Mary Magdalene were the only two people who were present at the death, burial and the resurrection of Jesus.

According to tradition he was the first Bishop of Jerusalem and the historians Eusebius and Hegesippus both wrote that he was martyred by the Jews in Jerusalem in the Spring of 62 AD.

Jude (Thaddaeus) is thought to have preached in Judea; Samaria, Libya and Persia, but according to tradition he also evangelised in Edessa and Beirut. Jude is believed to have been axed to death in Beirut, the Roman province in Syria, in 65 AD, along with Simon the Zealot and his remains are held in the same tomb as those of Simon in St Peter's Basilica.

Simon the Zealot was from Galilee and unfortunately very little is known of him, but the Eastern Orthodox Church holds that he was the bridegroom at the wedding feast at Cana where Jesus changed the water into wine. The most common tradition is that Simon preached in Egypt before joining Jude in Persia and it's likely that Simon and Jude were martyred together in Beirut.

Apart from the apostles, there were many other evangelists who were prepared to face martyrdom for preaching that Jesus had risen from the dead.

Stephen was a deacon in the early church who preached in Jerusalem without fear and who worked some miracles there as well. However it didn't take long for his activities to come to the attention of the elders and he was dragged before the Sanhedrin, where false charges of blasphemy were made against him.

Stephen was stoned to death outside the city walls of Jerusalem and Saul, later to be named Paul, approved of his execution and even looked after the clothes of those who were stoning him.

He was buried in the village of Caphar Gamla near Jerusalem and it's believed that he was buried with Nicodemus, the rabbi Gamaliel (who had educated Saul) and Gamaliel's son, Abibos.

His killing marked the start of a great persecution by Jews against the members of the early church, who were then scattered throughout the region.

Luke the author of the gospel and the Acts of the Apostles is thought to have been a physician and in Colossians 4:14 Paul wrote: 'Our dear friend Luke, the doctor and Demas send greetings.'

Some suggest that he may have studied medicine at the school of Tarsus where it's possible that he met Saul. Luke is thought to have been a Greek and not a Jew and he would therefore have had an excellent knowledge of the Septuagint and if he was Greek then this would make him the only non Jewish author of the whole New Testament.

Luke joined Paul and Barnabus at Troas (Turkey) about 51 AD and the three men later preached together in Macedonia. Later he was evangelising with Paul and Silas in Philippi (Greece) when Paul and Silas were both arrested and briefly imprisoned there.

On their release from prison, Paul and Silas left Philippi, but it seems that Luke stayed behind and he may have supported the early church in this city until 58 AD when he again joined Paul in Troas.

Luke was also present when Paul raised a young man named Eutychus from death.

They later travelled through Tyre and Caesarea together on their way to Jerusalem where Paul was arrested once again and taken back to a prison in Caesarea for two years.

It's thought that Luke visited him often in captivity and that it was at this time that he wrote his gospel and he may also have helped Paul write his letter to the Hebrews during this period.

When Paul appealed for his case to be heard by Caesar, Luke travelled with him on his journey through Crete and they were shipwrecked off the coast of Malta where they lived together for three months.

They then travelled to Rome, where Paul was imprisoned and kept under house arrest for two more years from about 61 to 63 AD, and again Luke spent a great deal of time with Paul and he may have written Acts during this two year period.

Not much is known of Luke after Paul's first term in prison in Rome but he was clearly with Paul again when he was imprisoned in Rome for the second time and he stayed with him until his execution.

There's a tradition that he was martyred in Greece but this is unclear and there's also an earlier tradition that Luke died peacefully, aged 84 in Boeotia, Greece.

Mark the Evangelist was one of the seventy disciples that Jesus sent out to spread the word in Judea during the early part of his ministry. His mother Mary was a respected member of the early church in Jerusalem and it was to her house that Peter fled after his escape from prison.

Mark evangelised with Peter for some time and he visited Rome with him, which is possibly where he wrote his gospel. There's a tradition that Mark wrote down the sermons that Peter gave and that these later formed the basis for that gospel.

Mark travelled with Paul and Barnabus from Jerusalem to Antioch around 45 to 46 AD and he also accompanied them to Cyprus and to Perga (south west Turkey) but for some reason he returned to Jerusalem when Paul and Barnabus left for Antioch.

This would later result in a dispute between Paul and Barnabus, as Paul refused to take Mark along with him on his second missionary journey. Paul and Barnabus split up as a result of this argument and Mark then travelled with Barnabus to Cyprus.

Not much is known about Mark's activities from this time until ten years later, but Mark is thought to have founded the church in Alexandria.

By 59 to 61 AD, Mark was clearly back in Rome preaching and Paul wrote warmly of him in his letter to the Colossians, so they'd obviously put their differences behind them by then!

It's thought that Mark also preached in Asia Minor and he must have spent time in Ephesus after his period in Rome as Paul wrote to Timothy and asked him to bring him back.

It's possible that Mark was also in Rome at the time that Paul was martyred, around 67-68 AD. However Eusebius wrote that Annianus succeeded Mark as Bishop of Alexandria in the eighth year of Nero, which was 62 or 63 AD, so he may have died around this time. There's also a tradition held by the Coptic Church that he was martyred in 68 AD by being dragged through the streets of Alexandria with a rope tied around his neck.

Saul was born in Tarsus and was raised as a Pharisee in Jerusalem under the instruction of Gamaliel and he was either a tent-maker or the maker of the fabric used for the tents. Saul was very active in the Jewish persecution of the early church that started with the killing of Stephen.

Acts 9:1: Meanwhile, Saul was still breathing out murderous threats against the Lord's disciples. He went to the high priest and asked him for letters to the synagogues in Damascus, so that if he found any there who belonged to the Way, whether men or women, he might take them as prisoners to Jerusalem.

However his beliefs were shattered when he experienced a vision on his journey to Damascus and after being blinded for three days he was baptised by Ananias and then spent several days with the disciples. He soon began preaching in the name of Jesus before having to flee from the Jews who very nearly killed him.

Paul then went into Arabia, probably in the region to the south of Damascus but unfortunately there's no record of his activities there. After this he returned to Damascus and three years later he went to Jerusalem where he stayed with the apostle Peter for fifteen days and on this trip he also met the apostle James.

Paul went on three missionary journeys, travelling to most of the major cities throughout the Mediterranean region and Asia Minor and he established several churches along the way. The first journey began in Antioch and he preached there with Barnabus for a year. Mark later joined Paul but only travelled with him for a short time before returning to Jerusalem.

In Lystra, Paul healed a man who'd been paralysed since birth which amazed the crowds to the point that they believed Paul and Barnabus were their Gods Hermes and Zeus! The Jews however stirred up the crowd, who angrily turned on Paul and stoned him, before dragging him out of the city and leaving him lying on the ground for dead.

Paul set out on his second mission with Silas and was later joined by Timothy and finally also by Luke. It was in Philippi that Paul exorcised a slave girl who could predict the future and who subsequently lost her powers as a result of the exorcism.

The handlers of the slave girl were enraged as they'd lost the source of their income and so they convinced a crowd to attack Paul and Silas, who were then stripped, beaten and severely flogged, before being thrown into prison. The two evangelists miraculously escaped after an earthquake damaged the prison walls.

Paul then preached for a short time in Athens before going on to Corinth where he lived for at least 18 months, starting around 50 AD. Initially he preached in the synagogue every Sabbath and the rest of the time he made tents, but when Silas and Timothy arrived he gave up the tent making and resumed preaching full time.

Paul's third journey began at Ephesus in Turkey where he lived for about three years and he was accompanied by both Timothy and Luke on this mission. Paul taught in the synagogue for three months and then began teaching daily at the famous lecture hall of Tyrannus to both Jews and Greeks and he's accredited with having worked many miracles during his time at Ephesus, as is clear from Acts 19:11.

'God did extraordinary miracles through Paul, so that even handkerchiefs and aprons that had touched him were taken to the sick and their illnesses were cured.'

However a riot in Ephesus forced him to leave the city and he then travelled through Macedonia to Troas in Turkey. Here a young man named Eutychus who had been listening to Paul preaching, fell to his death from a third floor window and Paul performed a miracle by raising him back to life.

After leaving Troas he travelled all the way back to Jerusalem, where a week later a mob tried to kill him, but he was rescued and brought before the Sanhedrin. He was then escorted by 470 Roman soldiers to Caesarea to stand trial and here he was imprisoned for another two years.

Paul appealed to Caesar and was sent to Rome for trial but en route he was shipwrecked off Malta where he stayed for three months with Luke. In Rome he was sentenced to two years house arrest but he was allowed to preach from this house and it's possible that after his release he may have visited Spain, as it's clear from his letter to the Romans that he had plans to travel there. (Romans 15:24).

If he did visit Spain then he may later have travelled back to the East, before again returning to Rome where he was imprisoned for the second time, until he was beheaded around 67-68 AD at Tre Fontane in Rome.

Paul described the incredible trials he suffered in the name of Jesus in 2 Corinthians 11:23:

"I have worked much harder, been in prison more frequently, been flogged more severely, and been exposed to death again and again. Five times I received from the Jews the forty lashes minus one. Three times I was beaten with rods, once I was stoned, three times I was shipwrecked, I spent a night and a day in the open sea, I have been constantly on the move."

Paul's thirty year ministry made a huge impact on the establishment of the early church and also on church doctrine to this day.

The above martyrs represent a few of the followers of Jesus who were prepared to leave their families, to endure enormous hardships and ultimately to face execution for preaching that he was the Christ.

The question has to be asked why would they have done this unless they were totally convinced that Jesus had risen from the dead?

What other explanation is there? If these men had known that the resurrection was a hoax then it's surely irrational for them to have spent the rest of their lives enduring terrible hardship, preaching that he was the Son of God.

However, if the risen Jesus did appear to them and even eat and drink with them over a period of forty days, before being taken up into the sky outside Bethany, then their actions were entirely logical.

So the behaviour of the apostles after the resurrection is the sixth piece of evidence pointing to the divinity of Jesus.

- Chapter 14 -
Reviewing the evidence - Was Jesus the Messiah?

There's surely no more fundamental a question than this, because if Jesus did rise from the dead then he is the Son of God and it would lend enormous weight to everything that he taught in his three year ministry. These are some of the statements made by Jesus about the importance of believing in him.

John 6:40: For my Father's will is that everyone who looks to the Son and believes in him shall have eternal life, and I will raise him up at the last day.

John 3:16: For God so loved the world that he gave his one and only Son, that whoever believes in him shall not perish but have eternal life. For God did not send his Son into the world to condemn the world, but to save the world through him. Whoever believes in him is not condemned, but whoever does not believe stands condemned already because he has not believed in the name of God's one and only Son.

John 6:51: "I am the living bread that came down from heaven. If anyone eats of this bread, he will live for ever. This bread is my flesh, which I will give for the life of the world."

Then the Jews began to argue sharply among themselves, "How can this man give us his flesh to eat?"

Jesus said to them, "I tell you the truth, unless you eat the flesh of the Son of Man and drink his blood, you have no life in you. Whoever eats my flesh and drinks my blood has eternal life, and I will raise him up at the last day.

For my flesh is real food and my blood is real drink. Whoever eats my flesh and drinks my blood remains in me, and I in him. Just as the living Father sent me and I live because of the Father, so the one who feeds on me will live because of me. This is the bread that came down from heaven."

Luke 12:8: I tell you, whoever acknowledges me before men, the Son of Man will also acknowledge him before the angels of God. But he who disowns me before men will be disowned before the angels of God.

The six pieces of evidence

First piece of evidence: The Messianic prophecies

These are the prophecies regarding the Messiah that were written between five hundred and one thousand years before his birth, from King David through to Zechariah.

These were all fulfilled in the life of Jesus, including the place of his birth; that he would be born to a virgin; that he would be betrayed for thirty pieces of silver, crucified and die for our sins and that his body would not see decay.

About a thousand years before Jesus lived, King David wrote that they would pierce his hands and feet and cast lots for his clothing, which is utterly remarkable as the first historical reference to crucifixion was 450 to 500 years later. What was the chance of this prophecy coming true in the person of Jesus?

Before 700 BC, Micah foretold that the Messiah would be born in the tiny and insignificant village of Bethlehem. Even 700 years later when Jesus was born, the population is estimated to have been between 300 and 1000 people. Again, what was the probability of this prediction being correct?

Isaiah predicted before 680 BC that the Messiah would be born of a virgin, would be pierced for our transgressions and be given a grave with the rich.

He also predicted that the eyes of the blind would be opened; the ears of the deaf unstopped, that the lame would leap like a deer and that the mute tongue would shout for joy. What were the chances of him making all these predictions about Jesus correctly?

Zechariah prophesied around 520 BC that the Lord would be priced at thirty pieces of silver and that they would be thrown into the house of the Lord to the potter.

This was precisely what happened as Jesus was betrayed by Judas for thirty pieces of silver. Judas later returned and threw them on the floor of the temple and they were used to buy the Potter's field as a burial place for foreigners. What was the chance of this prophecy also being fulfilled in Jesus?

Taken singly these prophecies would be remarkable enough, but what is the probability of all these ancient prophecies being manifest simultaneously in the person of Jesus?

Second piece of evidence: The miracles worked by Jesus

The miracles worked by Jesus are simply unprecedented in human history and were also described by non-Christian historians from antiquity.

They include hundreds of healings of incurable diseases and conditions such as blindness and paralysis and his ability to control the elements of nature itself, such as the calming of a storm and his ability to walk on water.

They also include the miracles of multiplication at the feeding of the five thousand and the four thousand and his greatest miracle, the raising of Lazarus to life after he'd been buried for four days, as well as the raising to life of two other people from the dead.

The miracles attributed to Jesus in the writings of both Christian and non-Christian writers cannot be explained by science and even today paraplegics and blind people cannot be cured, nor can a dead person be brought back to life four days after death.

After Lazarus was raised from the dead, the chief priests and the Pharisees were convinced that everyone would believe in him unless he was stopped. This was because the miracles were absolutely staggering to witness!

Third piece of evidence: Inexplicable darkness and earthquake

The phenomena associated with his crucifixion and death such as the earthquake, the darkness that covered the land for about three hours during the middle of the day and the tearing in two of the massive curtain in the temple, cannot be scientifically explained.

How could all these events have happened simultaneously at this one specific day in history? Objectively the probability of an earthquake and a total solar eclipse happening on precisely the day in history that Jesus was crucified is 1 in 4.7 billion.

And yet scientific analysis shows that this darkness couldn't possibly have been caused by either a lunar or a solar eclipse. It's important to remember that these events were also described by reputable historians from antiquity such as Tertullian and Phlegon. In the absence of a credible scientific explanation for this period of total darkness in the middle of the day, we must conclude that it was indeed a supernatural event.

Fourth piece of evidence: A guarded tomb found empty

Several hypotheses have been advanced to explain how the tomb of Jesus could have been found empty on the Sunday morning, despite it being placed under a heavy Roman guard and none of these provide a credible explanation for the empty tomb.

There was no motive for the Sanhedrin, for Pilate, or for the apostles to have stolen the body of Jesus and it's telling that some of the ancient historians also wrote that Jesus had risen from the dead. So after having discounted all the hypotheses, we're again left with the only plausible explanation, which is that this was also a supernatural event and Jesus did emerge alive from that tomb.

Fifth piece of evidence: Post resurrection appearances

Jesus is recorded as having made multiple appearances after his death over a period of forty days, including appearing to over five hundred people simultaneously. The resurrection of Jesus was also described by historians such as Josephus, Tertullian and Justin the Martyr and not just by the gospel writers themselves.

Sixth piece of evidence: Disciples prepared for martyrdom

What prompted such a radical change in the behaviour of all these men after the death of Jesus? The apostles had deserted him in the Garden of Gethsemane and with the exception of John, none of them were present at his crucifixion. Yet immediately after Pentecost they bravely went out into the streets preaching that Jesus had risen from the dead. What could possibly have motivated them to fearlessly preach the risen Jesus and to willingly die a martyr's death?

Conclusion

It's evident from Matthew's gospel that Jesus stated clearly at his trial before Caiaphas and the Sanhedrin that he was the Son of God.

Matthew 26:63: The high priest said to him, "I charge you under oath by the living God: Tell us if you are the Christ, the Son of God."

"Yes, it is as you say," Jesus replied.

And on the day he drove the money changers and traders out of the Temple of Jerusalem, when he was asked for a miraculous sign to prove his authority, his reply was specific and measureable.

John 2:18: Then the Jews demanded of him, "What miraculous sign can you show us to prove your authority to do all this?"

Jesus answered them, "Destroy this temple, and I will raise it again in three days."

So here Jesus was saying quite clearly that his resurrection would be the acid test to prove that he was the Messiah.

The startling miracle of the raising of Lazarus from the dead at Bethany, showed the Jews that he had power over life itself and this was surely a precursor for the resurrection.

We've carefully examined six pieces of evidence, which are remarkable enough when viewed independently of each other. But when pieced together, the evidence is overwhelming and leads to only one viable conclusion:

Jesus did rise from the dead and is therefore the Son of God.

Printed in Great Britain
by Amazon